THE

GLUMLOT

LETTERS

A Devil's Discourse on
Sobriety, Recovery and
the Twelve Steps of
Alcoholics Anonymous

Stanley M.

Publisher's Cataloging-in-Publication Data

M., Stanley
    The Glumlot Letters: a devil's discourse on sobriety,
recovery and the twelve steps of Alcoholics Anonymous /
by Stanley M.
      p.   cm.
    ISBN 0-9659672-3-9
    1. Alcoholics Anonymous—Humor.   2. Alcoholics
Anonymous—Fiction.   3. Alcoholism—Rehabilitation—
Miscellanea.   I. Title.
    HV5279   362.292   97-92399

Capizon Publishing, Box 3272, Torrance, CA 90510

Printed in the U.S.A., on acid-free paper.

First printing, September, 1997

03 02 01 00 99 98   9 8 7 6 5 4 3 2 1

Contents

Preface

These letters were written by a spirit we would call a devil. As a class, if I may use that word, these demons are liars and cheats to begin with, and the author of these particular letters appears to have no compunction whatsoever about plagiarism. Credits and references are almost uniformly omitted and items appearing in quotations may or may not be true to the original passage cited. I will not conjecture if this is artistic license, carelessness, or deliberate thievery. It is also very possible that this is part of their standard style or required form.

The reader is also advised that the chronological relationship of events as seen from the tempter's perspective is not anything like what we experience as the passage of time. I can offer no explanation and I did not even attempt to reconcile the differences.

So, I have passed along the letters exactly as I found them, with only one modification. On pages where I was able to determine and identify a specific human source of information or a quotation, I have included a reference number which is detailed in Appendix I. It is likely that I missed a good many other items in my review of the text and I apologize to anyone aggrieved by my oversight. Any corrections brought to my attention will be gladly rectified at the first opportunity.

Conforming to precedence, I shall not disclose the means by which these documents came into my possession. There are no particular or unique skills required other than patience and an ability to contend with abysmal penmanship.

As mentioned, the devils are not known for their honesty, but they may also be just as vulnerable to self-delusion and denial as any human. So I will leave it to each reader to sort out what is fact, fiction, and fancy within these letters. I hope that in his own way, twisted as it may be, Glumlot is able to carry a message of value to someone.

I would not want to be so presumptuous as to imply there is any required reading as a precedent to this volume, but it is my opinion that there are two titles the reader may want to consider as background material. The first is *Alcoholics Anonymous*, (the "Big Book") published by A.A. World Services, Inc. which is directly and indirectly referenced throughout the accompanying documents. The Twelve Steps of A.A., frequently mentioned and quoted in Glumlot's letters, are listed in full in Appendix II. The many references to other passages from the "Big Book" are enumerated in Appendix III. The other book that a reader may find of interest is *The Screwtape Letters* by C.S. Lewis. It was the inspiration for my acquisition of the collection of correspondence that follows.

Stanley M.

"But we aren't a glum lot....
We absolutely insist on enjoying life."

—from the book *Alcoholics Anonymous*, page 132.

Letter One

Dear Twigmold,

I received your letter and it was great to hear from you again. I couldn't help but notice your exuberance that your human had become a drunkard. That's all well and good, but it may not come to much.

Perhaps you did not know this, but I had the good fortune of being a student in the academy when the noted Tempter Emeritus, Snuffwick, did a series of lectures. He devoted several sections to drunkenness and sobriety, and I took very good notes. On occasion, I even consulted with him when several of my "patients," as he would call them, had episodes of alcoholic behavior—both drunk and sober.

I would like to share with you a few of the things I learned, in hopes you can avoid the common pitfalls and be prepared to take advantage of opportunities that will surely present themselves.

First off, as tempters for the underworld of the Lowerarchy we must always maintain sight of our objective: to bring souls to Our Father Below. Drinking is no particular sin. Nor is the act of abstinence any particular virtue.

The fact is many people don't drink at all and most of those who do imbibe, drink very infrequently and consume only small quantities. They are poured a glass with a liquored beverage at holiday parties or weddings and will wander around with it in hand. They might sip at it, but will eventually set it down and forget about it. Nothing we can make of that. Then there are those who have a few drinks and then stop when they start to "feel it." Now and then you can get a fellow to have too many and embarrass himself to some degree, but unless it progresses to a stage where he begins to despair, there is little value in it for us.

There are those who see drinking as evil. (Even though it was the Enemy's invention, we shall be happy to take credit for it.) They intentionally do not drink because it gives them a strong sense of moral superiority. This is very good. Snuffwick always pointed out that pride, and especially spiritual pride, was a wonderful foundation for building up smugness and ego. The inevitable fall from such heights is a delight to see, especially when they tumble right down to the foot of the table and look up to see Our Father Below. Ha!

Now, back to your fellow. You must tell me more about him. You imply he is drinking excessively. This may only be a phase. Many humans have such an experience, and most of them outgrow it. Merely drinking too much on occasion means almost nothing. What is important is what the patient thinks about it. We must always remember the vital question for us is, whether your charge is moving toward the Enemy or away from Him. This is the only thing that matters. It is of no consequence what other thing he is headed toward, so long as it is away from that, which to us, is the blinding eternal light of truth, mercy, and goodness. It is too ghastly to even think about.

If your patient is a loner and prone to maudlin self-pity, you can easily nudge him farther in the direction of melancholy and sullenness. It will isolate him even more and pretty soon you can suggest all sorts of things to distort his perception. Since we are not really able to create anything—that is the Enemy's invention and domain—all we can do is make suggestions that twist things one way or another. While it may be the patient's morose and unpleasant nature that drives people away—get him to place the blame on "them." Suggest a few drinks and it will amplify the noise already in his head. You need only to start playing it back to him. If he buys into it, then you can plant the idea that "they" are really the evil ones out to do him harm. This is a great tool, because as you take a more prominent place, he will become even less likely to sense your presence. Be prepared, though, to distract him if he starts to think about who "they" really are, for the truth of this illusion might come to him.

Now, you must realize the whole time you are whispering in one ear, the Enemy has agents posted on the other side. Our biggest problem is that we can't quite make out what these other spirits are saying to the patient. The best you can do is listen closely to your man's thoughts and you might be able to figure it out.

If your fellow is the gregarious, outgoing type, a few drinks may push him to being loud, obnoxious, and boring. These types often start out seeking companionship and approval as a way of countering self-doubt. They may be bright and sharp-witted when sober, but a human with a good sense of humor can be like poison to us. They will just as often find our subtle suggestions laughable, and that type of laughter, like music, is the work of the Enemy and is to be discouraged in our patients. But after a few drinks, we can get hold of the sense of proportion, and by twisting the self-doubt into self-assurance, the sharp wit becomes a sharp tongue and the humor's edge begins to cut too deeply and friendships can be seriously damaged.

Still, this by itself is of no great benefit, but it is the effect it has on the patient that can aid our cause. In any event, if it distances him from other people—this is very favorable. Often when the Enemy wants to get a message through to a human, the agents may use the indirect method, which is through another human. We have not been able to consistently duplicate this process (outside of politics) but the research department claims to be working on it. Please don't think I am criticizing them. I am fully aware of the Lowerarchy's policy on disparaging remarks. I was merely pointing out the certainty of their eventual success. Right? Good!

So the fact that your fellow drinks is good news only so far as the potential opportunities that might come about from it. The odds are not always in your favor, but you must leave no stone unturned. This kind of dedication and thoroughness will assure your demotion to lower and lower positions of authority and status in the Labyrinth of Hell's Eternal Lowerarchy.

Please write and give me more detail about your patient and his drinking.

Your friend,
Glumlot

Letter Two

Dear Twigmold,

It is interesting to hear your questions about whether or not your fellow is having blackouts during his drinking. I feel compelled to warn you that rather than anticipating this as a success, you may have entered an area that requires careful management. Remember, we are the salesmen from Hell. No high-pressure tactics will ever succeed. The real skill is the slow, steady, imperceptible distancing of our patients from contact with the Enemy. The best tempters will spend years in the trenches, gently tugging the unwary human along toward the gates of Hades.

There is some dispute regarding the source of the term "blackout," but there is agreement that it is based on the premise that blackness is the absence of light. I have been working out a way to verify if a patient is in a blackout, and I think it would be interesting if you were to try it and see if it works for you.

My proposal is that there are two specific criteria for a blackout. The first indication is the absence of shadows. (I am referring here to those shadows that are unique to the spiritual realm, not the ones found in the physical world.) Shadows need light, and all that is light, especially the blinding, all-knowing and eternal type, is the work of the Enemy. A shadow is normally cast when we are able to find something within the patient we can use to block that light. Where there are no shadows, you can be reasonably sure the Enemy is thoroughly, albeit temporarily, obscured. Our dilemma is that we cannot look at the light, and our mythology is filled with tragic stories of the demise of good tempters who gazed at the evaporating luminescence. So, the shadows are *our* dominion. And a blackout is our free range. It doesn't matter one bit whether it is caused by blind drunkenness or blind rage.

The second indication of a blackout is the temporary suspension of rational judgment that can be verified by a simple test: suggest an action to your patient that he would unequivocally reject under normal circumstances. If your fellow goes along with the idea, then you can be fairly certain you have a blackout.

When you are at this point, you need to be keenly aware of a number of factors. Foremost is to avoid the temptation (yes, we can fall victim to our own traps) to overdo things in this entertaining and unfettered playground. If you have worked with your patient long enough to be absolutely, positively certain his soul will be yours, then you may go ahead and have him drive his car into a bridge abutment, wrap it around a telephone pole, or whatever opportunities your imagination finds. With practice, you can get the timing just right and bring him out of the blackout at the very last possible moment. This would be the ideal time to make your appearance. The terror and horror will be magnificent. In the final split second, he will realize—too late—what he has done and your role in it. Ah, that is the eternally delectable icing on the cake. Oh my, yes that is enticing, isn't it? Where was I? Oh yes, if there must be innocent victims, be sure to follow the standard practice that only those who are irretrievably in the Enemy's clutches are to be the ones. These are humans who have been abandoned as utterly hopeless by their assigned tempters and are always surrounded by that bright, impenetrable cloud of the Enemy's presence.

But that is all end-game strategy. What you really want to accomplish in the early blackouts is to bring about an action that leaves some trace for the patient to encounter the following morning when the episode is over. Preferably something he would find stupid, disgusting, or humiliating.

If your man lives alone, and tends to drink in large quantities, then the wet bed is very effective. He is the only one who knows, and now he has a secret, and a constant fear of when it might happen again. These secrets isolate him from other people, and you have a great head start.

If the patient is a bar drinker, you can disrupt his equilibrium just enough so that he stumbles and bumps into to the wrong person—say a large, hostile biker, preferably also drunk. A short fight could yield a black eye or some other embarrassingly visible and painful damage. The patient now must fabricate a lie to explain away the bruises. This will isolate him from others, from himself and hence from the Enemy—all in our favor again.

If the drinker is a family man, you must be a little more judicious. He need only say a few hurtful words to his spouse or children to make the next morning silently and icily uncomfortable. If it lasts for days, so much the better. Remember, you want gradual but consistent progress. You will generally want to avoid extremes in these cases. Waking up in jail, or the threat of separation or divorce could shake a man into honestly wanting to change. Now, if the spouse is in the hands of an effective tempter, you may have more latitude. She may be strongly in denial and willing to take on the full weight of family secrets.

Your patient's family may have a more dynamic range to work with. Some tempters will even team up to take such a couple to very twisted excesses, such as screaming fights, thrown dishes, physical beatings, and the like. The actual deeds are not that important. You can achieve just as much with isolation and silence as with violence and noise. It is all a matter of style, I suppose.

Not all blackouts will yield opportunities such as I have described. Many just get totally ridiculous. These have far too many of the essential elements of an actual sense of humor—another of the Enemy's abominable creations—for us to get close enough to the patient to do any real damage. There are also anecdotal accounts of the Enemy's meddling with patients during blackouts—protecting them from themselves and from us.

Other blackouts are inherently uneventful, but this does not mean we are without methods. One of my favorite tactics for the morning after a blackout is to plant the suggestion, "You ought to go inspect the car." A quick jab to the imagination and you can have him checking the bumpers for damage, looking for grizzly remnants of things too horrible to think about. Humans will retain these totally fictitious mental pictures, which we can then drag up later. The emotional wear and tear is nearly as good as if it had actually happened, without the risks of real guilt and remorse that might prompt a patient to change. So you see, once again, the action is virtually irrelevant to our goals.

So, you want to avoid stirring up too much during your drinker's blackouts. The car crashes, the confrontations with police, and other high-drama situations give rise to self-pity, remorse, and self-condemnation, which are all good paving stones for the road to Hell. However, never forget the Enemy is going to be there in the morning also. These events can just as easily be the foundation upon which an Enemy agent would build repentance. A slight over-estimate on your part can destroy all your hard work.

Your friend—Glumlot

Letter Three

Dear Twigmold,

It sounds as if your fellow is having some serious concerns about his drinking and you imply this is undoubtedly the work of the Enemy agent posted at the other ear. I want to caution you against over-reacting. As I said in my last letter, any extreme circumstance can be used just as effectively by the Enemy as by you. They are often better prepared and their methods are better suited to high-intensity situations.

We are, regrettably, the underdogs in this battle between Heaven and Hell. We cannot create anything. The other camp has exclusive rights there. We are limited to making subtle suggestions, which a human may choose to totally ignore. It is only through good luck that he hears your suggestion over the din of the wretched and revoltingly sweet music from the other side. If he does hear your message, there is always the chance the Enemy will sense it and send an equal and opposite suggestion. If your idea has made it this far, the human still has the choice of acting upon it or not. If he does pursue it, all we have really done is set a wheel in motion. We have initiated a course of events, which we can optimistically hope will persist long enough to add to a state of spiritual unbalance and unrest. It is merely one shot fired in one battle of the one great and eternal war.

Once the chain of events begins, we have no real control over the outcome. We can try to out-shout the Enemy while the human moves along through his perception of the sequential nature of time peculiar to his physical and temporal existence. But each shout has to go through all the same obstacles: Does he hear it? Does he ignore it or accept it? Will he act on it? Extreme input will have wildly extreme and unpredictable outcomes. These are just as likely to drive the fellow toward the Enemy's camp. That is why I say slow and steady is always the better way. You want him far beyond the point of no return long before he has any clue what has happened.

Another tool, which I have observed senior tempters employ with impressive deftness, is the twist of perception. It is really the combined application of several skills, sometimes simultaneously, sometimes sequentially. Timing is everything. Obviously, as spirits, we exist outside of time as humans see it, so this is a talent that requires considerable practice, and can be mastered only through repeated trial and error. However, as we both know, the Lowerarchy imposes a limit on the number of errors allowed.

Of the tempters I know and with whom I have worked, the one who best uses this skill is probably Muddlesham. He had a fellow drinking at the bar. The Enemy agent seemed to be complaining to the patient that he was drinking excessively. Muddlesham moved to counter this by directing the fellow's attention to his own reflection in the bar mirror. The drunk dizzily said to himself, half aloud, "Hell, I haven't had any more than that guy!" The patient passed out shortly thereafter and retained no recollection of his close brush with the Enemy.

Muddlesham's other classic case was a patient who had become very isolated in his drinking, and in whom Muddlesham was building a rather substantial state of paranoia. In an attempt to discredit the fear, an Enemy agent coaxed the fellow out of his apartment to venture into the world and be with people. After a walking a few blocks, the man accepted his tempter's suggestion that a drink would ease the discomfort he was feeling. Muddlesham got the patient into the nearest tavern, and directed him to a stool at the end of the bar. However, the man did not realize he had taken a seat that put him just below the line of sight of the television, which was showing a popular sporting event. As he finally screwed up the courage to look around the bar, all he could see was everyone staring at him. Panicked, he ran out of the bar and has not been seen publicly since.

Another method that works with drinkers is a variation of the bait and switch. If the fellow has been drinking scotch and is getting into trouble, suggest that he switch to beer. "You'll get full before you get drunk." If he is a bar drinker, have him change pubs. "It's those people you've been drinking with." Better wine, smaller glasses, more ice, with or without food, the list is endless. The idea is to keep him focused outward—keep him thinking that his problem is external. All he needs to do is get the right combination and all will be well. This kind of self-delusion is very productive, provided it is allowed to progress in very small increments. Too drastic a shift and it could wake a sense of self-awareness and the man may begin see the illogic of your scheme.

One variation of the perceptive twist is actually a spin-off of the children's game of opposites. If he is with people, suggest that he'd rather be alone. You can easily find something at hand to reinforce this. They are boring and he is not; they are not drinking and he's thirsty; it's too warm in here and a cold one sounds good. If he is by himself for the moment, draw his attention to it. Ask your question in such a way as to bring out the negative: "Why are you all alone?" You see?

If he is with family, then long-standing, unresolved resentments can provide a plethora of choices. There is always the old reliable one: to whatever the spouse says, ask him, "Yes, but what does she *really* mean?"

A more sophisticated version of this, where timing skills are critical, relates to the human's non-verbal communication. Some tempters foolishly pass over this opportunity entirely. Remember, a human is part spirit. This is the part we are most interested in. The rest of him is animal, and is, I admit, rather repulsive. Nonetheless, it is an area where much can be accomplished. Pay close attention to his reactions to a sideways glance, or a raised eyebrow, folded arms and such, and you can get him to center his response on that, rather than what was actually said. You can also do equally well by distorting his perception of a vocal inflection or an emphasized word. This will, as often as not, lead to a miscommunication, then a misunderstanding, then hurt feelings and so on.

It matters not if the end point is fear, anger, self-pity, or remorse. If it distances him from other people, then it distances him from the Enemy, and it is another brick in the wall between the patient and the light. Take it in stride as a small victory.

I must express my concern about your patient on one particular matter. If you have overheard thoughts where he is questioning his drinking, is he just having mild doubts or was he directed by the Enemy to engage in true self-searching and self-examination? This could be a dreadful setback if you don't handle things carefully. If it looks as if he might actually quit, make sure he is prepared to give the Enemy no credit for it. Let him think he is doing it all by himself. Your voice must be full of loud congratulations. In a few days or weeks or whatever, you may find him thinking back on his drinking, "It wasn't that bad." You must act quickly and agree enthusiastically. Suggest that since it has been a while, he can surely have a few without danger now. Better yet, tell him he deserves a drink for his accomplishment.

You are probably pondering an obvious question: "Is your man an alcoholic?" The answer is—we don't know. Since much of it is a physical disease, and we have no access to that realm, we cannot know. However, there are strong indicators, if you know what to watch and what to listen for.

The fact that your man is wondering about his drinking may be a clue. Normal drinkers rarely wonder about their alcohol consumption. When your patient is contemplating his drinking, you might try a few preposterous or impossible suggestions, like the bait and switch, for example. If he unhesitatingly buys into a ludicrous proposition, he may be an alcoholic. After all, only an alcoholic would agree that changing jobs, or changing brands, or changing sleeping partners could solve a severe drinking problem. Of course you run the risk that if he is not a practicing alcoholic, he will laugh at your suggestion.

There is also what the humans refer to as the spiritual side of the disease. It is, at least as far as we have been able to determine, little more than a slightly enlarged spiritual capacity. You see, all the research and intelligence data indicate the Enemy produces nearly all of these human creatures one-hundred percent complete. None of them have the same one-hundred percent, mind you, but hardly a one has been short-changed. Some have looks, some have brains.

Some have artistic potential, others are good at math. Some can have a drink or two, now and then, without danger. Others are missing certain physical attributes, which render them deathly allergic to alcohol, in conjunction with a mental quirk that manifests as an obsession to drink. The humans in this group are over-sensitive and self-centered, but they also received an extra dose of awareness of their spiritual potential. Unfortunately this capacity, if unchecked, spills over into things like love and a sense of humor. Both of which are lethal to us.

The mental aspects and resulting physical action of the disease are absurdly easy for us to work with and capitalize upon. Keep your patient in the problem and the prospects will remain hopeful. Well, do keep me posted.

Your friend,
Glumlot

Letter Four

Dear Twigmold,

I received your urgent letter. So your patient has been invited to an Alcoholics Anonymous meeting and what should you do? For Hell's sake, don't panic. No situation is as bad as it seems. If you go into it with an all-is-lost attitude, then you will be the one lost!

If you are going to be successful, you will follow the path of all the great tempters. Use the skills you have learned and make the most of each situation to wrench the patient away from the truth, light, and freedom, and move him closer to the banquet table for Our Father Below.

I have attended many of these A.A. meetings—more than I would care to admit—and the key to success is being quick and precise in using the basic techniques of distraction, befuddlement and fear. Remember, humans live in time. Temporary change can be a pleasant diversion, an annoying distraction, or even momentarily traumatic. But the specter of permanent change is often truly and totally terrifying. A.A. opens the door to complete change. Most certainly for the worse from our point of view, but get your patient to see only the door—not what's on the other side—and he may never step across the threshold.

Before I go into detail, I am obligated to warn you of the potential danger of accompanying your fellow to a meeting. It is possible that one or more of the humans in attendance are in very close contact with the Enemy. They will be surrounded by that impenetrable light upon which we must not even glance. But do not be discouraged. Many meetings are conducted without these folks present.

Obviously, we would rather not have your patient attend at all. Suggest watching a lurid or suspenseful television drama. Chances are he does not really want to go an A.A. meeting anyway, so you will find your fellow rather receptive. If he feels that he must go, try to get him to botch the directions and become lost. Then he must decide whether to forge ahead and arrive at the meeting late. Ask him if he wants to draw attention to himself. Capitalize on his natural fear of the unknown with the specter of the "unforgivable gaffe." Suggest they have very strict rules about tardiness, and he would have to stay late and write something over and over again on a chalkboard. Tell him there are many other similar regulations which he could violate. He might clumsily infringe upon one and then every person in the room would know he is new. In some meetings, the seating seems to be pre-assigned, so your man runs the risk of taking the chair of some important officer or revered elder. Work with him along these lines and I bet he will gladly turn around and go home. Or better yet, straight to the nearest bar.

He may, despite your efforts, still end up in the meeting. Make sure he gets some coffee right away. The coffee is always bad and the pastries are usually stale. Let this be his first impression. If he is at all shaky, have him spill his coffee. He'll be embarrassed and retreat into awkward self-consciousness, thereby emotionally separating him from the other humans. Suggest he avoid eye contact. This will also help keep him isolated.

Since most meetings are a real mix of people, have him notice the differences. You will find a lot of material available. Age is usually an obvious one; gender is good; you may even find possibilities with race or style of clothing. You can easily find ways to make him see himself as not fitting in. Either he is the wrong color or they are. They will seem much younger or very, very old. If your man feels he is overdressed, tell him he is obviously of a superior class. If he has the opposite feeling, tell him they all notice it, too, and are judging him accordingly. Suggest that the laughter he hears may be at his expense. Whatever the circumstance, his mind will be racing and you only need to listen carefully to find your mark.

Now if someone does approach your patient, this is where the real craft comes into play. You must have your patient fully notice the uncomfortable and un-pleasant feelings and aspects of the interaction without absorbing any of the content of the message. If the approaching individual is from the Enemy camp, you will need to keep the patient completely distracted. Most probably, the person speaking to your patient will be different in some apparent way, so emphasize that difference. As long as it is not one of the Enemy's folks, you have little to do or worry about. You will find that your patient's general anxiety will automatically obscure every other word. Turn up the noise level on this and it can generate real fear.

As he is waiting for the meeting to start, and before everyone else sits down, have him look around at the other people. Draw his attention to the fact that he is seeing something he does not often see elsewhere—men hugging men. If you can arrange it, have some of these folks sit on either side of your patient. The mental squirming will be delightful.

Now as various people read and speak in accordance with the format of the meeting, prepare to shift your patient's attention. When a member is reading aloud from their book, make certain he hears all the sentences with the word "God," especially if he has any negative religious biases. Have him casually sneak a few glances at the people around him. Ask him how he could possibly have anything in common with these people. Have him take in the more abnormal physical features and appearances. The large ears on this fellow, that woman's double chins, the fellow (or girl) with all the tattoos, the old man's wrinkles, the youngster with the odd-colored hair, the immense bottom on that person, and so forth.

See to it your fellow pays attention when a member begins to whine and ramble on and on and on about a broken shoelace or some such nonsense. There is always an abundance of this at most meetings. However, if one of the few who really does have the answer begins to speak, quickly divert your patient's attention and have him start reading through the Steps, which are likely to be posted on the wall. Suggest to him, "This is pretty drastic and extreme stuff." If you are unable to keep his focus away from the speaker, suggest to him, "This must be a cult."

Oh, I forgot to mention one of the other seating strategies. Some tempters lead their patients to sit in the very back of the room near the exit. This does allow for a quick or early departure, but the more experienced A.A. members have learned our trick and now regularly patrol these areas for "newcomers." You will also want to avoid the very front rows because there is less material for distraction.

Most meetings will ask the newcomers to introduce themselves to the group. You must ardently recommend to your patient that he *not* do this. If you have been working diligently up to this point, then your suggestion will be warmly received. Tell him, "This was all a mistake, why make it any worse? You're not like these people anyway." If he is really pressed by one of the glad-handed greeters, have him give a fictitious name.

At the end of the meeting they will probably stand up, hold hands, and recite a prayer in unison. While it is very little like real prayer, it is similar enough, with the aura-like cloud of the Enemy's presence, to render the humans virtually unapproachable. Of course when it is over, you are there whispering in your patient's ear. Give him the idea this is just a cover for a religious organization. If your man envisions himself sophisticated, have him see this as really hokey and really wonderful for "them," but it doesn't apply to him. If he is the paranoid type, suggest this is all fake; that there is some ulterior motive. Fire his imagination and you'll have him picturing himself as a missionary in the deep jungle, or as a shaved-headed, orange-robed monk with vows of poverty and—egad—chastity!

One of my finer triumphs was the patient who attended two different meetings in the same week. One was his very first A.A. meeting. The other turned out to be a recruitment drive for a multi-level marketing plan. In both groups everyone was nicely dressed, a speaker told an inspired success story, and each wanted him to continue to attend meetings. He was pretty certain the soap sellers were after his money. He wasn't quite so sure about A.A., though. Maybe they wanted him to sell God. But where was the money angle? I said, "Oh, I bet you are right. There has to be a catch somewhere."

He returned to neither and continues on his way down the slippery slope to Our Father's fiery dominion.

Your friend,
Glumlot

Letter Five

Dear Twigmold,

It appears that I should have discussed the slogan "keep coming back" in my previous report. Alcoholics Anonymous is rife with such pithy propaganda. But the point of my last letter was not to give you a specific, fool-proof game plan. Actually, it was quite the opposite. The point I was trying to make is that you can, at least in theory, twist anything around, including these wretched slogans, as long as you are prepared to act quickly.

Look for the opportunities. The fact your fellow has decided to attend a few more meetings only gives you additional chances to discourage him. If he attends one where they recognize the achievement of various lengths of sobriety, tell him he could never get that number of days or years. If this doesn't work, tell him, "These people probably didn't drink the way you did, that's why they can go so long without one." Or there is always the old standby, "They're all liars."

You also need to understand some of the mechanics of the human mind and what repetition can do. With things the patient enjoys, like a favorite song, hearing it again and again reinforces a pleasant experience. For something he does not like, such as a coworker telling the same war story for the tenth time, the mind becomes desensitized and starts to tune out the input. If there is something the patient really dislikes, say, the voice of a nagging wife or the whining of a spoiled child, he can be prompted into anger.

In applying the effects of repetition to his A.A. attendance, the next time he is thinking of going to a meeting have him picture the same people, telling the same stories, reading the same passages, eating the same cookies. Remind him how boring, how brutally boring it is. Ask what will become of him if he continues to attend. Will he become boring, too? If he is at a meeting, every time someone says, "Keep coming back," have him repeat it to himself mockingly with a squeaky, high-pitched, sing-song voice. It will store in his mind that way and become more irritating every time he hears it.

At most meetings, they read part of Chapter Five from their book. After only a few repetitions we can start to numb the mind and lull it into wandering. Before long, you can get the mind to automatically shut down completely upon hearing the opening phrase, "Rarely have we seen a person fail...."

In this way we begin to build up a wall against the Enemy's onslaught even while the patient seems most vulnerable. If he has attended meetings for any length of time, and you can get him to skip one, you need to lean on him hard. "Well, you missed a meeting and nothing happened. You didn't drink. See, it was easy—

no big deal. Maybe you weren't that bad after all. Feels good to be free of those boring meetings. Free, yes! Why, this is cause for celebration." If you have been doing the footwork, then it will be you who gets to celebrate.

Once he has a drink, or a "slip" as the A.A. people call it (like it was an accident), you have several directions you can take things. If your man is at all the depressive type, plant the idea that he tried A.A. and it didn't work. While going to a few meetings is not the same as working the program, let him think he gave it a fair shot. If he is the prideful variety, which is very common, let his imagination run with the thought, "I can't go back now. What will they think? How could I face them?" If he is the angry, hostile sort in whom you have made fear the center of everything, his drinking bout can be a stage from which he can shout curses to A.A. and all "those" people.

This is not to say all who attend the meetings eventually turn back to drinking. Some do. But don't think you are off the hook if this happens to your patient. There are classic cases where such episodes have driven a person back into A.A., but with a new willingness, honesty, and dedication that is sickeningly repulsive. If a human attends a few A.A. meetings, you want him to have only enough of the message to spoil his drinking—just a little. Not enough to make him really want to quit drinking. Remember the old rule: we want him paying an ever-increasing price for an ever-diminishing return. But this needs to happen so slowly he does not notice it. If you can make his experience in A.A. permanently sour his drinking and still have him despair of ever recovering, that would be ideal.

While the Enemy is restricted to working with the truth, we actually have a more interesting tool kit. Certainly we have our area of specialization—the lie. The truth comes in only one flavor, but with the lie, ah, we have a veritable cornucopia. There is the mild little white lie. "Oh yes, dear, you look lovely in that dress." A human will convince himself the white lie does no real harm. (They forget what a few drops of water started at the Grand Canyon!) There is the sweet tang of the clever deception, which might cause a little incidental damage. But that damage pales before the gains we achieve from the teller's swollen pride and ego at having "pulled it off." Then there is the common fib—pungent and intense. The value here is from the eroding fear that ensues with the risk of getting caught. Finally there is self-delusion for the ultimate in a bold and enduring taste.

My personal favorite is making the truth sound like a lie. There's a certain panache to it, don't you think? "The newcomer is the most important person in the meeting." Right. And the turkey is the most important guest at the Thanksgiving table. "Keep coming back." Why? Because we're not through with you.

There is always the grim possibility your patient will actually enjoy the meetings. The Enemy tries to set this up, but you will want to use this momentum to push the patient *farther* in that direction. Eventually you can get him completely off track. Have him view the phrase, "Keep coming back," as implying that he will, in short order, become a circuit speaker with all the appropriate prestige and status the A.A. people seem to attach to it.

If your fellow is asked to read something from the standard liturgy, you should hope it is the one with all the unpronounceable "anonymities" in it. Most newcomers fumble this word without our help, and you can convert excitement into embarrassment, and pride into humiliation.

Another tack is to point out one of the many apparent contradictions, yet keeping him from seeing it as merely being a valid paradox. You can easily guide him through a logical argument along these lines: "They say 'one day at a time' and then they turn around and celebrate the anniversary of someone's sobriety date. That is hypocrisy!" Or, "They say 'one day at time' but they mean *forever*." Once you have your patient running with this you can pull in his ego. "They must think you are stupid to not see through this flimsy veil of deceit!"

Often the truth can be painful. That's our "in." These human creatures will go to any length to avoid pain. The exceptions are those patients we have gotten to the point where they are used to pain, in which case they will fight to keep it. This is only because whatever they presently have is familiar. Change is not a big deal, but the *thought* of change can be threatening and painful. The unknown might hurt. Therefore, avoid any possible *real* change.

The A.A. program is all about change. Each little truth your patient hears in a meeting will be a pin-prick of discomfort. Make sure he feels each one. Let the pain distract him so as to dull the recording of the truths he hears. Let the pain be the predominant message. Sharpen the senses and try to make it cumulative. So, the truth can work in your favor if you know how to frame it. The truth is not an end in itself, as the Enemy claims it to be. The truth is a means to an end. Everything is to be used to bend the patient's will away from the Enemy. If something can't be taken advantage of, if it can't be exploited, then what use is it?

Finally, whether your fellow relapses into drinking or not, make certain you direct his attention to the advertising of alcoholic beverages in the popular media. This has been our home turf in the Great Battle, and we have held this ground almost since the beginning of the daily popular press. We have many of our best minds working here and they are masters at making lies seem like the truths. The humans who appear in the ads are always healthy and happy. They are young and successful. They are bright-eyed and sincere. I have absolutely no idea how our associates have been able to pull this off so successfully for so long. You never see any bleary-eyed, vomiting drunks in these ads, do you?

——Glumlot

Letter Six

Dear Twigmold.

It is very unfortunate that your patient seems to be so serious about attending more meetings. I assume you have been interfering with his sleep. The normal discomforts of chemical withdrawal will aid this for a few days or weeks at the most. Beyond that, you must be there when his head hits the pillow to start the non-stop, high-speed, chain-reaction thinking. Keep his mind going seven different directions at once. If he feels rested then *you* are the one who has been sleeping on the job! And given the demands the Lowerarchy places on us to deliver souls, I am sure you will not want to draw undue attention to yourself in that fashion.

If your patient keeps going to A.A. and you are not otherwise able to distract him, he will eventually come across the question of getting a sponsor. First, try to dissuade him from thinking he needs any help. If he is at all self-centered and egotistical, encourage him to think, "I am smart enough to figure out all this stuff on my own" or "I would rather do it my own way." If he as exhibited reservations about any of the Steps, reinforce them by suggesting he doesn't really need a sponsor because obviously not all the Steps apply to him. An even better ploy can be found in the fact that in nearly every geographic region there are "names" given to the subordinate in the relationship with a sponsor. In some areas they are called pigeons or babies. You can easily use the negative connotations of these terms, plus the patient's pride, as good reasons for him to exempt himself.

The categories of sponsorship seem to be without any formal structure, but there are some relatively common and predictable types. There is the "meeting buddy"—fairly harmless unless it develops into true friendship. There is the "let's go for coffee after the meeting" sponsor, who will introduce your patient to the fellowship only, and the coffee will keep your patient awake long into the night, leaving him exhausted the next morning. There is the service addict—all activity but no action. He will have your man stacking chairs or setting out the literature or buying the cake and cookies. The risk here is that the service work keeps them around long enough to be exposed to those A.A. members who have been heavily influenced by the Enemy. Another type is the "call me every day" sponsor, who will come across as being dictatorial and too structured, so he will intimidate and chase off most newcomers. There are also the book thumpers, page-number quoters and bleeding deacons.

The ones that must be avoided are the actual Step-working sponsors. These come in three groups: One would tell your man, "Work the Steps and tell me how it goes." This is the least dangerous, because it leaves you to help the patient guide himself through the process. (Yes, through the process and out the door!) The second group will tell the new fellow how to work the Steps. However, since most alcoholics hate being told what to do, you can leverage this tendency into either passive inaction or vehement rebellion. The final group represents the greatest and most perilous threat to you and your patient. Under the direct influence of Enemy agents, they take the neophyte through the book and show him how they worked the Steps with the help of their sponsors. They provide compassionate guidance and encouragement along the entire way. The thought of this would send shivers down my spine—if I had one. The good news is that this type of sponsor is fairly rare. We don't know exactly how they snag their victims, but the chances of your patient falling prey to one of this group is remote, so it ought not be terribly worrisome for you.

If your fellow is bent on getting a sponsor, then you need to manage the selection process as best you can. I had a patient select a man for a sponsor because the gentleman wore a classy watch. That's a good reason, isn't it? Alternatively, have him set unrealistic criteria for a "perfect" sponsor. Since such a fellow does not exist, this will drag out the process, and delay is good. Have him look for the ideal parent. Cultivate the idea that the sponsor he is looking for will be there to give him constant, unconditional approval and meet each of his unspoken emotional needs. Find a reputable tempter (well, yes this is an oxymoron, but you know what I mean) and combine your efforts, and surely you can find the A.A. member who considers himself the "ideal" sponsor. Match up your man with this pompous, self-righteous chap, who clearly has no answer, and there's a good chance it would lead one or even both of them into disillusionment, anger and drunkenness. Have your patient find one who does fellowship, friendship, and coffee but would not encourage your man to do any serious work with the Steps. If he gravitates toward the more dangerous type, have him pick one who is too busy to really give any help. As a last resort, mention to your patient that the word "sponsor" does not appear anywhere in the first part of the A.A. book.

The official qualifications for sponsorship are, as far as I can tell, a very closely guarded secret. One would think length of sobriety is an important prerequisite for the job—given all the attention they give to celebrating days and months and years—but there does not seem to be a specified minimum. The length of sobriety only means an individual has been successful at staying away from the first drink for a period of time. If this is *all* he has done, and he has done it by sheer willpower, determination, or fear, this could be a fine sponsor for your patient. If he accomplished it by actually working the Steps, have your man look elsewhere.

See if you can find one who is around ten or eleven months sober. These are the ones who are often on fire with enthusiasm, but little else. If he doesn't scare your man off with his intensity, then the chances are slim that he has had anything more than superficial experience working the Steps. The back-up position with this type is that in a few months he will hit the post-anniversary depression and enter the "Is this all there is?" phase. His disillusion may be contagious, and could add to the discouragement you've been feeding to the patient. Also, make sure the prospective sponsor does not have a sponsor himself.

Find one who is inexperienced—who has not sponsored anyone before. Not realizing how much work and commitment are involved, he will be so enthralled by the prestige and honor of finally securing the lofty status of being a sponsor that nothing serious will happen with your patient.

In most circumstances, a human's impulsive decisions are good for us, but I would strongly recommend you avoid this with regard to selecting a sponsor. The Enemy's teamwork is, well, much better than ours. Your man could get caught by that disgusting and devious little deception the Enemy's agents love to pull: the coincidence. Your patient could be matched with the completely wrong type of sponsor.

Assuming your patient ends up with an acceptable sponsor, make sure he does nothing further. If he starts to consider taking any action, remind him that the expression he hears repeatedly is, "Get a sponsor." It doesn't say any more than that, does it? Now that he has a sponsor, the task is complete. Finished. The obligation fulfilled. Compliment him on how well he has done to have met this goal. Then have him neglect to call, or be too timid to pick up the phone. If an issue does come up, tell him "You don't want to bother your sponsor with this itty-bitty little problem, do you? What would he think?"

Your situation may not be as bad as it seems. Just remember that old maxim, "The fastest runner is brought to a halt by a pebble in his shoe."

OK, so it isn't an old saying. I just made it up.

Your friend,
Glumlot

P.S. I hope you know that I am not being serious about making up that haiku or whatever it is. I know full well that kind of conduct would make me guilty of being creative, and I assure you that I am constitutionally incapable of that. I am certain that I must have heard it or read it somewhere before.

Letter Seven

Dear Twigmold,

It seems your patient's selection of a sponsor was more in the hands of the Enemy than we would have liked. I was able to gather some information on the fellow and you, my good friend, have your work cut out for you. The sponsor's tempter is Grimsnore. I suggest you contact him and start coordinating your efforts. (But do be cautious in your dealings with him. There was talk that he once served up another tempter in order to meet his quota.)

In the meantime, I will share with you what I know about A.A.'s First Step. The sponsor of the type that your patient just happened to select, will very probably encourage your chap to look at the book and the Steps. Your man will be asked to start on a course of action, and we would prefer him to stay on a course of thinking. All action takes place in the "now," and that is the Enemy's most fortified encampment. We want your patient all wrapped up in either the past or the future. Keep him away from "Now," and you keep him away from "Him."

The Step in question is the one that asks them to admit they are powerless over alcohol and that their lives have become unmanageable. Obvious as it may be to everyone around him, for a real alcoholic to come to this conclusion can be exceedingly difficult. Keep it difficult and things should improve. There is a fairly predictable process that can be circumvented with a nominal amount of planning.

The stories they tell are intended to allow the newcomer to find common ground within A.A. Upon the basis of a shared or similar experience, the newcomer is supposed to have less resistance to acknowledging his alcoholism. We are not sure how, but this does seem to work for some patients. If he enjoys the stories he hears in meetings, assure him they are fine for their entertainment value, but are not worth much else. I assume that you have enough sense to keep him out of the book. However, if he does read it, have him see the stories in it as old and outdated.

I have to tell you how I was able to chase one patient out after his first encounter with A.A. He was referred to a nearby meeting. As his attendance was obligatory, he went but was very uncertain and skeptical. The noise in his own head made my job quite easy, but I cleared the channel only long enough for him to hear one story. It was told by a fellow with whom the patient had virtually nothing in common. It was narrated in a humorless monotone and was all drunkalogue with no message of hope or recovery. After the meeting, the group took my patient out for coffee, and I was able to seat him next to the very same fellow, who proceeded to tell my patient the exact same story almost word for word! From that day on, the patient steadfastly maintained his first and only impression of A.A.: for these sad and sorry folks, somehow the endless recitation of one's drinking experience is what keeps them sober.

If your chap does relate to a story, start him on the "Yes, but..." train of thought. It doesn't matter if his experience is milder or worse, just different will do. You can dredge up one of the more disgusting or horrendous things he did while drinking and ask him to imagine himself telling this piece of his history from the podium. Imply that he will *have* to tell it. That ought to do the trick. He will probably become faint and queasy.

If your patient persists, the next strategy is to make Step One seem really simple. Have him see only the physical aspect—the drunkenness—but not the mental or spiritual sides. Befuddlement through simplification. Ah, yes, now that's style. Tell him, "By gosh, they are probably right, just stay away from the first drink and you won't get drunk. You have the answer now. Why do you need to keep going to meetings?"

Another reason to keep him out of the book is the section near the beginning, the part written by the doctor. It discusses the physical and medical aspects, and labels alcoholism as a disease. I tell my patients that introductions and prefaces and forwards are all superfluous and contain no useful information. They can be skipped over entirely. If he does pick up the book, you ought to be able to play on his imagined intellectual superiority and his know-it-all-ism to have your man go straight to Chapter One.

If he does latch on to the disease concept, have him visualize other physical maladies or injuries he has had, and how they have healed. (But try to avoid any images of serious deformity or permanent disfigurement, as this is far too close to the truth of alcoholism.) Keep it limited to things like, "You got over the mumps, didn't you?" This can lead your fellow back to the bar in no time at all.

His sponsor may direct him to some of the fundamental concepts of Step One in the book. In that case, suggest that his powerlessness was the *result* of extreme drunkenness, not the cause. Disconnect it from anything having to do with his inability to avoid the first drink and therefore all subsequent ones. At most, you would like him to buy the idea that he was powerless over the fifth or sixth drink. Make sure to give the word "powerless" a bitter taste. Equate it with weak, feeble, and helpless. Make it sound languid and feminine. Get him to remember the good times, and ask him, "How could they call that powerless?" Better yet, have him associate powerlessness with impotence.

If he does take the first half of this step, remember that change is inevitable and nothing is permanent. Sooner or later the time will come when he will not be able to come up with an argument against your suggestion of, "Oh, surely you can have just one." Some humans say "slip" is an acronym for sobriety looses its priority. How about Satan laughs in perpetuity? Oh, if they only knew.

All right. Back to business. The second half of the step, "...that our lives had become unmanageable," was one of our crowning achievements. We had one of our finest tempters, Snuffwick, on full battle alert during the original writing of the Steps. He fought against grossly unfair odds in the proximity of that foul sweetness and blinding light. Our advocate was not able to impair the content of the Enemy's message very much, but he was able to muddle the language on the second half of this step (and several others). As we are not privy to the Enemy's communications with the humans, we don't know exactly what would have been written, but the general consensus is it turned out well for us. This is a classic example of making the most of bad situation. Let me tell you why.

I've not run into many A.A.s who are willing to concede to the powerlessness in the *second half* of Step One. The ego automatically rebels against it, and we are there in full array with drums pounding noisily in total support. The deceit here is to shelter the patient in the shadow of the illusion that his life was ever manageable in the first place. This is automatically simplified for us because most humans think the word manageable is synonymous with malleable—a resolvable situation that will yield to persistent persuasion. They think that something manageable is eminently do-able.

Actually, the word manageable means "easily controlled." Clearly, human beings have little control over the phenomenal world and the other people in it. The only control they have and the only control that matters, is of the choices they make. We do our best to obscure this conspicuous truth, but the role of choice as it pertains to the spiritual realm is another matter entirely. Our prime task is to have the humans see the physical world as the only place where they really are, and where they ought to be masters of all they see. Of course, very little goes their way, so we push the emotions to the other extreme and they see themselves as failures or victims. From that point they are now justified to exert themselves even harder, or plan their vindictive retaliation, or fall into hopelessness and self-pity.

Under your guidance, your patient can probably come up with a number of examples of how his life *is* manageable. He may still have a job, a house, a family, a car, a watch that runs, or most of his own teeth. Whatever. Keep telling him these physical items are hard evidence that this step, or at least the second half, does not apply to him. If he can skimp here, then it will be fine for him to pick and choose from among the other things the program suggests, right? If you suspect the Enemy of drawing his attention to the passage in the book which says "half measures availed us nothing," don't let your patient interpret that it means "half-*steps* availed us nothing." My favorite counterattack here is to quietly suggest that if a half measure avails nothing, then a ninety-nine percent measure should yield just about twice as much. (Don't let him do the math, though.) An alternative is to remind him that in school seventy percent was a passing grade and anything above ninety percent earned an "A." So, on average he ought to be able to half-step a few and still get by.

I can imagine you are asking yourself, "Why go to such bother to divert a patient from the Steps?" First let me clear up a common misconception. The Steps are not really as distinct and discrete as one might guess. It is more a gradual and continual process. It is more like an inclined plane. I sometimes wish we could have gotten that concept in the book instead. How about, "Here is the ramp we have ascended...." That would turn off a newcomer, wouldn't it? And a "ramp" makes backsliding sound less treacherous and more inevitable. Anyway, the second half of Step One is really the transition to the first half of Step Two.

There was a French novelist, another of those bipedal human animals with a name that even sounds like the bellow of animal—Camus—who wrote something I wish more of Hell's tempters understood. He said, "A man is always prey to his truths. Once he has admitted them, he cannot free himself from them."

Once an alcoholic concedes the fact of his condition, we cannot easily undo it. We cannot make it untrue. We cannot pry it loose from its moorings. Truths are like weeds. You can't get rid of them unless you get out the roots. Our problem is the roots of truth are always in Enemy soil, deep in Enemy soil. So, ours is a program of preventative maintenance. Our great, loud, blustery winds must keep the seeds of truth from ever taking hold.

In my study of humans, which is for academic and educational purposes only, I have yet to figure out why they overlook some blatantly obvious contradictions. For example, take the popular expression about how the truth shall set them free, (which is of Enemy origin) and the Camus quote I mentioned earlier, where they can never be free of the truth. Tell both of these to a human and he would nod and say, "Yes, yes, both statements are true." But clearly, they cannot be. Either the truth leads to freedom or to imprisonment. One or the other, but not both. Isn't it ridiculous that a human so easily misses the incongruity of it? I have no idea why the Enemy goes to such great efforts about such insipid and witless creatures. Then again, it may be that both statements really *are* false and this is all one of the Enemy's subtle little schemes to try to muddy up things and confuse us.

Do not assume that if a fellow has completed all of Step One that he is forever lost to us. While it would be foolish to deny this occasionally happens, it is by no means the rule. However, once exposed to A.A., and by that I mean the program of action in the Twelve Steps, the experience can really ruin an alcoholic's drinking. What usually happens is either he returns to the A.A.

program or he drinks himself to death. The problem
with a premature death is that it is, more often than
not, accidental. It can happen before we have completed
our work in securing a mortgage on the patient's soul.
The decedent's shock and surprise at the brutal truth of
his situation can immediately turn him toward the
light. We would rather see a slow, drawn-out, and
annoyingly painful death. Not excruciating pain, just
excruciatingly wearisome and tedious. Have the patient
absolutely certain that an unpleasant end of this sort
will occur, but with no idea how long it will take. The
longer it seems to last, the better the despair and
anguish.

The problem with the returnees to the program is
the increased probability they will accept the first few
steps eagerly and willingly. They have fresh, firsthand
knowledge and a clear understanding of the truth of
their disease. Since "a fact will fit with every other fact,
but a lie will not fit anything except another lie,"[1] keep
your man surrounded by your best work, and soon he
will cast aside all truth as being illogical.

I shall write again,
Glumlot

Letter Eight

Dear Twigmold,

In response to your request, I would be glad to provide more information about the Steps and how one might prepare for the perils and opportunities of working with a patient who is considering A.A. membership. If you are successful, do not hesitate to pass word along to your undervisors about the help I have given you. If you fail, it would only be your own fault and no one down there would listen to you anyway.

Forgive me if I state the obvious, but it is too easy to fall into the very traps we set for our patients. This can distract us from the simple basics we all learned in school. I organize these techniques for defending against the truth into three categories: a) avoid, b) obscure, or c) twist. The first—avoiding the truth—is usually harder initially, but has a more long-lasting impact. Keep the truth away from him, or him away from the truth. Either way works. Continually look for a lull in your patient's attentiveness in which to suggest, "Oh, you can skip *one* meeting. You've been doing so well." The next meeting after that will be even easier to skip. If he does go to a meeting, obscure the message at the critical moments and it will be almost as good as if he was not there at all. When he does hear some of the Enemy's message, take a word out of context, and twist it by digging up an old negative association or misunderstanding of the meaning of the word. Then you have a valid-sounding basis for proposing that he disregard the whole thing.

One formula that incorporates all three of these is to convince him he must intellectually accept the entire program as a prerequisite to beginning any work on the rest of the Steps. However, the Steps are not just an intellectual exercise. Acceptance comes as the result of *getting* results from working the Steps. So you see, the idea that he must buy into the whole program before he moves on to the next step—is practically impossible. To use human metaphors, we are really putting the cart before the horse, but we make it sound like the unanswerable question about which came first, the chicken or the egg. You would be amazed at how easily a human with any seeds of doubt about the A.A. program will buy into this ridiculous reasoning, but, hey, it works.

I wanted to write to you about the Second Step, "Came to believe that a Power greater than ourselves could restore us to sanity." This one is full of words that can be easily distorted in a human's thoughts. There is little reason any A.A. beginner should ever make it past this point. Let's take the word, "believe." Have your man see it with a capital "B." Believe, Belief. Make it sound very religious. Associate it with the word faith.

Toss in the sounds of a boisterous Saturday night revival meeting, or the soft punctuation of a monk's avowed silence made by the shuffling of worn and dusty sandals beneath his dark, hooded robe. Fashion in his mind that "belief" is intellectually radical and extreme, yet in application it is puritanical, dogmatic and boring. You get the idea? If nothing else, have him look it up in the dictionary and find it is between "belie" and "belittle." Suggest there must be a common meaning if these words are that close together.

It gets better. The next phrase is "a power greater than ourselves." Here, I would take the patient to a point of ego-centered self-righteousness with questions such as, "What kind of propaganda is this?" Point out that it is a thinly disguised ruse for the word "God." Tell him, "They must think you are a fool. If they mean God why don't they come out and say it? Probably because they are trying to hide something. Hmm, what could that be?" If his imagination doesn't immediately take off with this, dig up recollections and pictures of the people who used to knock on his door Saturday mornings, offering pamphlets about the end of the earth and salvation. Ask him if he is ready to spend all his free time doing this sort of thing.

Pay close attention to where his mind goes. You can gather a great deal of information about his fear and prejudice of religion. If nothing useful comes along on its own, there are a number of ideas you may want him to explore.

This Higher Power they are talking about, is it the God of the churches, the punishing and unforgiving God? What about the Greeks and Romans with their many gods? Couldn't they just as easily be right? If there is one God, then why are there Jews, Moslems, Christians, Hindus, and Buddhists? How can each claim to be right? Where do the holy rollers and the snake handlers fit in? Then there is the eastern religion where all of eternity is one cycle of breathing in and out by a deity. Who can make sense of that? What about all the atrocities, the wars, the genocides, the hypocrisy, and the apparently endless array of unreconcilable differences? Maybe there is a God out there, but what does He care about one individual human?

The last part of the step, "restore us to sanity," was another of our outstanding achievements. Here, just as in the writing of the First Step, our tempter on the scene was able to cloud the author's thinking just enough to botch the language. I don't know for certain, but my guess is the human who wrote the original first draft had studied Latin. He probably intended to convey the concept of "wholeness" or "completeness," and ended up with the word "sanity." In Latin, *sanitus* means soundness of mind. Now, in the physical world, a thing that is "sound" has structural integrity. Integrity means all the parts are there, in the proper proportion, they fit together and are properly attached in the right places.

The humans have an axiom stating that a thing is often greater than the sum of its parts. Luckily for us, the humans rarely apply this to themselves. They do not sense the potential for totality, for the "wholeness" that the Enemy desires for them. They may vaguely sense that He has a vested interest in their spiritual side, but the human perception of the spiritual realm is that it is, by its very nature, unreal. It is too different from their physical world to be regarded on equal basis—it is a separate thing. We, of course, vigorously promote and support this assumption. We will even help defend such a position to the death. We don't want them to be whole or complete in this sense. We want them to gradually, ever so slowly, fall apart into bite-size morsels. Mmmm—the very thought of it!

Anyway, most people (who either did not study Latin or slept through it) think of the word *sanity* as meaning the opposite of *insane*. To them, insane means crazy, berserk, or totally and irretrievably mad. So when your patient reads that a Power greater than himself can restore him to sanity, have him distinctly hear the implication that he is insane. He will most assuredly bristle with antagonism and resist the idea. Say to him, "These people are saying that you are nuts. This could not possibly be true. You did some crazy things while you were drinking, but you are not a strap-down, lock-up mental case. You are not confined to a padded cell. You are not sleeping in cardboard boxes. You have a job. You are allowed out and about to be around other people. Since this step obviously does not apply to you, then none the remaining ones do." During the meetings have him look around at the other people while you suggest, "Look at them. *Those* people are probably crazy, but not you."

If your patient bought into Step One, you can always derail him on Step Two by working him along the following logic: "A.A. has shown me that I got drunk a lot because I had trouble setting limits. I can see that now. Thank you very much for the information. Maybe now is a good time to start setting limits—because this insanity thing is too much. I am drawing the line here. Since I am not crazy, I am no longer qualified and there is no need to attend any more of these meetings. I am out of here."

The procedure is not as simple or easy as I have described it. It can often be a long, drawn-out process to take a patient through these twists of logic. Persistence is essential and you ought to be working your other approaches concurrently.

If your patient is susceptible to the God idea, you can use the obscuring techniques to get him off the track without him ever noticing you have done so. One of the more interesting ones involves using a variant of standard distraction. Have him choke on a cup of hot coffee or on one of those powdered-sugar donuts during a particularly quiet and serious part of a meeting. Then tell him, "That was a message from the Enemy. It is a sign—you are not supposed to be here. Apparently, God does not want you attending A.A. meetings."

However, this type of method does not always work.

This brings to mind one meeting where a human male was standing at the coffee counter, talking to a very attractive young lady. Meanwhile, we were talking to the man—about the girl, of course. We had him off in the future, distracted with some very graphic mental imagery of a possible intimate interaction. Eager to impress the young lady, the man leaned back against the counter and took on the most casual, nonchalant pose he could. He inadvertently backed sideways into the coffee spigot and the hot coffee was running straight into his pants pocket. Of course, by the time he noticed, the damage was done. His pride was hurt, he had sustained a minor but painful burn, and his pants were wet, which is always an attention-getter in a crowded A.A. meeting.

The unfair and sad ending was the patient walked away without giving us any credit. Well, that's not completely true. He didn't really walk, it was more like a limp-skip-limp. Anyway, he had the absurd thought that his "guardian angel" had something to do with it! He said it was the Enemy's sense of humor—an ironic message having to do with his being hot to get in the girl's pants. What is worse, as a result of this line of reasoning, he moved much closer to the Enemy, and we have made very little progress with the man since that incident.

The hard reality of it is, even when we do our best, things can go wrong. It is not that the Enemy's agents are better equipped. I am not sure that is even true.

We can lie, they cannot. We can manipulate and hide the truth, they cannot. They offer vague, intangible benefits. We offer immediate worldly pleasures. They have to play by the Enemy's rules. We do not. It is just that even with all these advantages, we still lose some of the battles. That is just the way it goes.

Oh, by the way, if your patient does spend any time reading from the book concerning the Second Step, be sure to read over his shoulder and catch the part about the "bedevilments." I was so surprised when I first saw it. It filled me with such pride. It is clearly a reverent tribute to our work. It recognizes nearly the whole range of our area of expertise, and clearly portrays the extent of our effect on humans when in the hands of a master tempter. Snuffwick must have been in fine form at the writing of that passage.

Your friend,
Glumlot

Letter Nine

Dear Twigmold,

From the remarks in your last letter, it is obvious that I should offer to clarify a difficult concept—human time. I have learned the human perception of time is one-dimensional and this limitation almost completely obscures their understanding of the spiritual plane. To the extent we can maintain their confusion, we ought to be able to keep them from any meaningful study of the spiritual realm.

The A.A.s have an expression, "One day at a time," which, from our view, seems rather ludicrous. I am not sure if the A.A. folks developed this phrase themselves or borrowed it. A great deal of what their program offers has been stolen from other sources, but don't waste your efforts trying to get them to feel guilty about it. For some inexplicable reason, not even our most experienced tempters have made any progress on this front. The Enemy commands them to not steal, yet turns around and aids their larcenous act by harboring the criminals in shameless ignorance. Duplicity and deceit had traditionally been our exclusive weapons. This whole thing just adds to my conviction that the Enemy is not the goody-goody He pretends to be. His proclamation of unconditional love for the humans has to be part of some clever scam, because it does not make any sense. The soul is like a cash crop, to be carefully tended, harvested when ripe, and offered up on the banquet table of Our Father Below. What else could it be good for?

The cliché, "One day at time" is actually a fair representation of the human experience of time. To your patient, time is sequential and unidirectional; it proceeds along a line that is divided into either the past or the future. "Now" is limited to the infinitesimal point where the past and future meet. More precisely it is the state of transition through which an unknowable future rushes to become an immutable past. It is a fleeting, ever-vanishing event of seemingly insignificant proportions compared to the expanse of an endless eternity.

Yet this same minuscule moment, less than a blink of an eye, this "now," is where all physical human experience occurs. The past and future are virtually irrelevant to spiritual matters. Since the humans are partially animals, their view of existence is pretty much limited to the physical plane. The past and future are experienced only as thought and never seem part of "now." These mental states stretch into the past as recollections or into the future as imagination.

Our aim is to have the patient spend as little time as possible in the present because that is precisely where the Enemy is. The Enemy has stated He is concerned with what the humans do. That is because their actions are always in the present—where He is.

We are concerned with what our patients think. Because thinking takes them into the past as memories, resentments, or remorse; or it flies off into the future as fear, anticipation, fantasy, and so forth. Take your patient out of the "now" and you move him away from the Enemy.

You see, there are really only two dimensions to the physical world: space and time, and the Enemy has supplied an infinite quantity of each. Then in a flip-flop of celestial proportion, He prefers that the humans disregard it all entirely. If a human is to consider the physical world in any regard, He asks that it be valued on a qualitative basis only. He would have them appreciate the simple beauty of a flower or the awesome majesty of the night sky. The Enemy is equally delighted when a human will spend even a few moments being kind or helpful to others—without any thought of material or physical reward.

So, we take the opposite position. It is quantity that matters. For physical things, the emphasis is on bigger, better, larger, more, more and always more. I'm sure you remember all the basic instructions on the use of greed, lust and gluttony from your academy classes, so I don't need to go into it here. In dealing with time, since we cannot change it, I find the best option is to distort the human perception of it. However, there are no hard and fast rules, so you have to take each case on its own, making your best judgment of how to handle each situation.

If your patient is engaged in some activity that you don't want him doing (such as attending A.A. meetings, listening to a newcomer, being of service to his family, and so forth) you should drag time out for as long as possible. The goal is to take it to the point of insufferable tedium. Try to get him started on a critical internal dialogue. "When is this going to be over? Aren't there are more important things to do with this time?" An interesting trick that I enjoy is the more often you can get him to look at his watch, the slower time goes. Try it. It works.

But the Enemy plays the time game, too. He will try for the kind of spiritually satisfying self-forgetting that draws the patient so totally into "now" that he loses all perception of time. The effect on the human is that the time will have passed, not just quickly, but completely unnoticed. There is usually an afterglow (the Enemy's equivalent of a hangover) that lingers on after the event is over. For as long as this noxious euphoria remains, you will find the patient effortlessly resistant to the distractions that worked only a few moments or hours before. However, as the fulfillment of this serenity fades away, you will find him returning to his same old self.

Ego satisfaction, however, is a different story. It is always rooted in either the past or the future: reliving prior conquests and glories, or else lost in fantasies of future achievements and recognition. Let him conjure up and bask in lavish praise and worshipful adulation for some great heroic deed. Play this make-believe story out to a happy ending and maybe he even gets the girl! Then you've got him by the imagination. You will want this kind of mental state to consume a lot of real time. But it should seem to go by very rapidly. And best of all, because it is only a state of mind, there is no action and therefore—no risk. The more time he spends here, in his head (with you), the more likely that reality will become bland and boring.

I recently read an engaging article from the D.E.P.T.H.S. of Hell (the Department of Ethereal, Physical, and Temporal Human Studies). These devils are always striving to lower the standards for academic papers, and they may have outdone themselves with this one. The article was about the links between space and time, and the peculiarities of certain astronomical phenomenon where infinite gravity causes infinite time. Anyway, its conclusion was, as spirits, we are without physical mass, which is why we seem to be exempt from the effects of time, gravity and terrestrial chronology.

As you know, the humans have made an exacting science of the study of the physical world, but not of the spiritual world. This has been our doing. The rule we impose (that scientists can study only what they can measure) was devised and established by the finest minds in our institutions of lower learning and was packaged as "modern scientific inquiry."

The whole premise behind this brilliant move is that anything measurable is "real" and everything else is "unreal." If it cannot be measured—from within the confines of the four dimensions of human experience—its existence cannot be proven. If it cannot be proven then it is tossed aside as subjective, hypothetical and not worthy of scientific study. The humans have such a great capacity for hubris and arrogance that they have maintained this assumption for us, with very little ongoing support from us. This kind of closed-mindedness stands as a natural barrier between man and the Enemy. That's fine by us.

The other natural barrier is the ego. The Enemy's creation of the human ego is widely seen from below as a strategic blunder of immense proportions. It is an error that we exploit ruthlessly. The Enemy wants the humans to choose sides. But He wants them to do it independently, so He gave them free will. For this to work, the humans needed a sense of individuality, so He gave them ego, which has only one purpose—it is the boundary between self and everything else. The problem turns out that the ego sees itself as the center, as the whole self, the entire being, essence and all.

We capitalize on this self-centeredness, and because of the Enemy's laisser-faire attitude, this is where we taste our sweetest victories. When your patient looks in a mirror, mostly what he sees is his skin, the outer boundary of his physical exterior. If you were to ask him if he thinks of his skin as his true self he would laugh at you and probably say it is only the bag that keeps his innards in. But suggest to him that his ego is a paper-thin transparent shell, or little more than a line drawn on a map, and the ego will jump in to deny and defend. I do hope you understand that I am speaking figuratively and the premise I offer is a theoretical example, an academic exercise. These questions should never actually be posed to a patient, for there is a risk he could realize the truth.

Combining the effects of terrestrial time, the physical world, and the ego, it is easy to keep your patient thinking the spiritual world is off in some remote, inaccessible place, or way out in some distant future. Tell him it could not possibly be "here and now." Let him believe that if he is "good," maybe he will go "there" someday, but not today. Not when you have so many more interesting, and fun things for him to do.

Your friend,
Glumlot

P.S. Heaven may be infinite, but Hell...is eternal.

Letter Ten

Dear Twigmold,

Thank you for providing a more detailed description of the drinking history of your patient. It sounds very much as if he qualifies for A.A., but it doesn't seem as though he is one of the really desperate, low-bottom ones. That is good news. I know that may sound odd, but the deeper the despair and hopelessness, the more likely the fellow would grasp onto the program from the very start. Of course we want them to be hopeless, but we don't want them to know it. Mildly miserable is fine, especially if it drags on for years and years. Save the absolute and utter blackness of futility for the very end, when it is far too late, and the exquisite conquest is yours. So if he has any doubt about this A.A. thing, find it. If there is any buried hope that someday, somehow, something will change so that he can drink again, protect it and nurture it.

I gather from your letter that he continues to work with his sponsor. If that is so, then a discussion of Step Three is in order. In the published edition of the Big Book, the Step reads, "Made a decision to turn our will and our lives over to the care of God *as we understood Him*." First, I ought to give credit to those tempters who worked so diligently with the early A.A. members as the book was being written. The original version of this text included turning things over "...to the care and direction of God...." Our agents were able to get the word "direction" taken out—a brilliant move. It left a huge hole through which many an A.A. has fallen. By watering down the language just this small degree, we allowed a foothold for the human ego.

The book mentions that an A.A. member will look for "...an easier, softer way." Most tempters learn to foster the illusion that anything familiar is easier, and things that are new will be difficult. A human has to put in the effort to learn the new thing. What if it is too hard to learn? Even if learned, what if it is too difficult to do? Difficult implies the possibility of failure. Failure is the foundation of rejection. Rejection leads to abandonment and so on. Of course the secret, the common thread in all of this is fear. And fear is not based in the present. Drag your patient's thoughts into an unknown future, and any one of a number of negative emotions will take it from there and run with it. Keep him out of "now," away from the Enemy. Keep him in thought and away from action. Otherwise you risk his finding out that doing the Enemy's will *is* the easier, softer way.

Let's look at the step in detail for its many inherent weaknesses that we can turn to good use. "Made a decision to turn...." The decision is the action part of the step, but you will want your patient to gloss over this and simplify the entire step into "turn it over." This phrase has become ingrained, through our help, as part of the standard vocabulary of A.A.-speak, even though it does not appear anywhere in the main part of their book. It is a frequent topic in meetings, which helps reinforce the distorted and simplified version of Step Three. Convince your man that "turn it over" is the action part of the step—and he will think he has actually done the Step. (And being that he hasn't, he will have problems doing the rest of the Steps.) Keep him away from the fact that a decision is inherently "now." If he starts to lean toward making a decision, have him make a resolution instead. To "resolve" is to be determined and committed about some future action, but it is not the action itself. A resolution postpones the decision, pushing it away from "now" and off into the future. Let your patient boast in his meetings that he "turned it" over in Step Three, when all he really did was give the possibility a brief mental consideration.

"...our will and our lives..." My guess is the original A.A. members saw this as so obvious as to require little elaboration. It refers to one's thinking and action. Action is always in the "now." By placing thinking in the Enemy's hands as the step would have them do, it also reverts to "now." With both segments (thinking and action) in the immediate present, they are subject to the Enemy's influence, and it is more likely the two will function together with integrity. Clearly this kind of unity should be thwarted at every possible opportunity. This is best done, as with most things, by pushing it off into the future. Bring up the old phrase "last will and testament" as a definition or an example of "will." Your man probably feels noticeably healthier now, so tell him this kind of morbid business about preparing for death is a long way off.

For "...our lives..." you can use much the same image—a long, long life. There is a subtle little trick of logic you can try. Since the present is over so quickly and life seems so long, you can assure your patient that more of his remaining life is in the future than in today; the majority of it, in fact. And majority rules, right? This may take him away from the truth that his life can only be lived in the present.

"...over to the care..." To humans, "care" is such a nice, warm, fuzzy word. Full of motherhood, concern and compassion. To be on the receiving end of care is to be without a care. It has nothing to do with action. All take and no give. That's why, as I noted earlier, the change from "...the care and direction..." to just "...the care..." in this step took away any implication that prayer was involved. Prayer and meditation are popular means of receiving of direction from Him. This could lead to action, which is following those directions. If your patient seriously looks at the word "care," tell him, "It means only that God Loves you." Either it will lull him to inaction, or it will make him nauseous. (It does me.)

The next phrase is "...of God...." If your patient is like a good many people, he will feel a degree of resistance to this word. It may be anywhere from mild annoyance to outright antagonism. Wherever you find him along this continuum, let him know he is justified in his position. Paint whatever images of the Enemy are necessary to keep the patient skeptical. Maintain the threat to the ego that "turning it over" means loss of control. Some in A.A. say that surrender is just moving over to the winning side, but you want to associate "surrender" with prisoners of war, bamboo cages, death camps—that sort of thing.

"...*as we understood Him.*" This concept can be good or bad, depending upon your patient's understanding of God. However, as a preliminary move, you may want try emphasizing the "we" as exclusionary, as in "us—not you." If your fellow has any abandonment issues or bad church experiences, this might work to set up a barrier around him. Let him think such a wall can keep God out. This is precisely the best way to use the ego. It will also reinforce the ego's belief that it is the central self. If he has not read the book, or you are able to keep him distracted while reading, you can imply this part of the step means he has to buy into *their* understanding, as opposed to his own conception as the book talks about.

The fact is most humans worship themselves or nothing at all.[2] If a human has any inkling of the spiritual plane, it will almost invariably be "out there," meaning external to himself. Because everything external is also physical and is likewise bound by the three spatial dimensions and time, any concept of God he finds here will only be a "mental image of God."[3] Maybe it is the one given to most children, the grandfatherly old graybeard in the flowing robe. Maybe it is his own, and possibly, a very sophisticated conception. But even those humans who have made such rudimentary spiritual progress are still limited to worshipping their image of God.

Your patient may have an idea of God with which he is comfortable. As long as it is not too close to the truth then you ought to keep him comfortable in it. It is familiar and therefore easier. You can even suggest to him that he has it right, and everyone else is wrong. A little spiritual pride and complacency can go a long way—in our direction. Eventually, you want him sufficiently dogmatic so as to become inflexible and unwilling to change his belief. The shadows will grow longer and longer as he moves away from the light.

Another of the clichés in A.A. is "Let go and let God." As long as you maintain the "letting go" relegated to physical and external things rather than internal thoughts, ideas, prejudices, and beliefs you can make fair use of the phrase. If you have been grooming your patient to be irresponsible, then this saying can be used to justify and rationalize continued sloth. If he is of a generally dark mood and gloomy temperament, then a resigned fatalism can be cultivated.

However, I think you ought to understand the truth of "letting go" if you are to be successful in defending your patient against it. One human writer pointed out that spiritual progress is "more relinquishment than acquisition."[4] At an A.A. meeting, I heard a member say, "I am a vessel of fixed capacity, and I am filled up with me. I cannot add anything until I make some room."[5]

You see, there are two kinds of people in the world: those who have found God and those who have not. Of those who have not, there are two kinds: those who are looking and those who are not.[6] There is little we can do with the first group. Of the second group, some of the seekers may be salvageable, and the rest of them are already ours.

One final thought on "turn it over." The truth is the patient cannot turn "it" over, because he does not have "it." Never had it, never will. He only owns the illusion. We made the down payment and we always make sure that the patient stays current with the mortgage, but it is still an illusion. The only thing he can turn over—is the illusion itself.

Your friend,
Glumlot

Letter Eleven

Dear Twigmold,

You sounded really discouraged about your patient continuing with the Steps. Oh, please! Your job is to bring that kind of negative emotionalism out of your patient, not the other way around. Besides, I hope you realize you are standing at one of the grand turning points. Your man is poised before Step Four! Look around. How many of the humans in A.A. really do this Step? The prospect of this one scares off as many new people as does the mention of God. Allow me to elaborate.

The first order of business is—as always—to talk him out of it. This is very easy to do. Ask him, "Is this really necessary?" Remind him that the A.A. book says the Steps are only suggestions, meaning he ought to be able to skip this one entirely, right? Point out that he wasn't all that bad. In his drinking he only hurt himself. He didn't do anything to harm anyone else, not really. Try the words "austere," or "draconian" with regard to Step Four and see if he doesn't agree with you. If he is strongly independent, ask him if he wants to give in to "peer pressure" from the group. If he has paranoid streak, tell him, "This is all a bunch of brainwashing."

Just a word of caution, though. Don't dwell on these excessively. The goal is to quickly build and reinforce his confidence that he has succeeded in rationally debunking the program and is now justified in turning away from it. The reason I say this? So you do not have to repeat my mistakes.

I had leaned pretty heavily on the cult and brainwashing point while appealing to a patient's sense of intellectual superiority. The error was in letting him go to the library to research the matter. He found out that A.A. does indeed have several characteristics in common with cults: repetition (Keep coming back) and a preoccupation with recruitment (twelfth step work). However, he learned it does *not* have the other characteristics, *all* of which are required to qualify as a cult: A.A. does not isolate its members (get a job, go back to school); most groups have no charismatic authority figures ("Our leaders are trusted servants"); and the accumulation of money and wealth is not an issue ("We are self-supporting..."). I could go on from this list, but the point is, by trying too hard, by being too clever, I managed only to out-smart myself. I had prodded the man into action. Perhaps this is why I now emphasize the slow, steady approach so much. I figure that by sharing it with you, I am reminding myself.

Another avenue for steering him away from Step Four is to make it seem very, very big. Too big. Point out that it leads to Step Five, where he must tell this stuff to another person. Certainly he has a secret he feels ought not be told to anyone. Have him get busy with other activities and maybe he can attend to this step at a more convenient time. Every postponement buys you time to work out the next angle.

If he has been staying sober, he will be doing better at his job. Or has actually gotten one. Let him be quite impressed with this kind of success. Pat him on the back and acknowledge this as *his* success. If things are improving economically, encourage him to become greedy or miserly. If he is regaining the respect of his coworkers, inform him that it is really their admiration, which he undoubtedly deserves; and that he is being humble by not demanding more from them. You can inspire him toward ambition, or let him coast into sloth. You get the idea?

If he insists on working the Fourth Step, have him do it poorly. Persuade him he can do it all by himself, but keep him out of the A.A. literature. There are plenty of other "guides" that have very little in common with the process as outlined in the book. Keep him obsessed with doing it "right." Have him focus on getting the form and format correct, rather than content. Tell him he can work this step without a sponsor's help. If your patient had chosen a better sponsor, one who had no experience working the Steps and who did not have a sponsor himself, then this wouldn't matter as much. When it comes to our patients working Steps, half measures avail us everything.

What is at risk? What is the downside? That he will

find out the truth. The truth that the demons he battles are not us, but his own beliefs—those long held, coddled, nurtured and protected, self-absorbed and delusional assumptions upon which he has built his precarious self-image. We have made him feel comfortable with his beliefs, and we have sheltered his convictions in shadows. We are not the contemptible villains portrayed in human art and myth. We are not evil. We are merely catalysts for a larger process. We are facilitators. We are farmers. No, that's not really the right analogy—we don't plant anything other than suggestions. We are more like gardeners; hired hands who tend to what is already growing. We use what meager resources are available to fertilize the soil and weed out the truth. We attend to the seedlings and shade these tender, delectable shoots from the Enemy's harsh and searing light.

If he wants to dabble with an inventory, try the following format: tell him he is not oversensitive, it is just self-directed empathy; he is not childish, he has a youthful mind; he is not greedy, just motivated to be self-sufficient; his manner isn't pompous and grandiose, he is self-confident; he is not inconsiderate, he is free from the obsession about what others think; he is not conceited, he has learned to love himself; he is not lustful, he just has an abundance of natural desires.

If his sponsor directs him to the Big Book, the two things in our advantage are the very clear way the instructions in the book were written, and how very complicated alcoholics make everything. These two facts just about guarantee that if your man dives in and uses the book by himself, chances are he will miss the point entirely, or he will become confused and discouraged, which puts the ball back in your court.

I would also urge you to keep your patient away from the dictionary. From your letters, I assume your patient speaks English. Fortunately, English is a mongrel language, with no coherent roots and very little consistent structure. The implied definitions of most words are learned in a conversational context and we have been quite successful in keeping that changing about every generation or so. We have gradually made the reading of serious literature quite unfashionable, and the popular media of your patient's time will maintain this status quo. Therefore, for most humans, a word may carry only a single, superficial implication or vague notion, but rarely a real definition.

For example, Step Four starts out by looking at resentments. Few beginners in A.A. could tell you what a resentment is, but will quickly assure you they don't have any. Humans call themselves sentient beings, from the Latin word *sentio*—to feel. So, resentment means to re-feel. Feelings are fine as long as they are directed inward, as in selfishness rather than outward as in compassion. We drag the patient into his past to re-feel a perceived injury in order to take him out of "now."

The best resentments are based on an implicit

assumption of privilege. The ego will readily supply you with these. The Enemy gave the humans self-esteem, which is the ability to hold opinions about themselves. Where possible, take it to an unrealistic extreme. Let your patient think he is far better or far worse than the people around him, then alternate back and forth between the two. Under the right conditions, you might even be able to achieve the ultimate in confusion and internal conflict by maintaining both the high and low opinions simultaneously. When other people don't act in accordance with the distorted self-image, there are only two options: either the self-image is wrong, or those other people are wrong. Out of fear of ridicule, the ego will drive the patient straight to the second choice. Once the perceived wrong is recorded, you can then take the patient back to replay, to re-feel the injustice done, thereby reinforcing the erroneous assumption that started the whole business.

Your patient may also hold contradictory beliefs. Of course, he won't sense the discrepancy, but his actions will confuse the people around him and distance them from him. You will find lots of good material from his childhood. The messages he received alternated from one end of the spectrum to the other. He was the good boy and deservedly spoiled, or else he was neglected and therefore unlovable. He was expected to excel at everything or he was told he was good for nothing. He was told to be a man and restrain his emotions, and then reprimanded for tormenting the cat.

Sorry, I've got to sign off. My patient just received a call to take a newcomer to a meeting. I need to ride along and harp on my patient about the inconvenience of it. The weather is bad, the meeting is too far away, this is interrupting his personal time, etc. With any luck the new fellow will be intoxicated and will not have bathed recently.

Your friend,
Glumlot

Letter Twelve

Dear Twigmold,

I think I left off in the first part of the Step Four inventory. While the step reads "Searching and fearless moral inventory...," I find it more effective to aim for a "scorching and clueless" one. Painful and pointless. It doesn't take much of that to turn the patient toward an easier, softer way.

Alcoholics are not all that different from most other humans. It is just that they are never emotionally in the middle of the road for very long. Their out-of-proportion ego is needed to counterbalance an out-of-proportion, low self-esteem.[7] This exaggerates their need for security and approval, which complicates their relations with other humans. Since the ego assumes it is always right, it becomes fairly easy for us to maintain a predictable equilibrium by bouncing the patient back and forth between these two extremes. The only thing that can threaten the precarious stability of this arrangement is the truth.

Let me run through a fairly standard scenario. Whenever something (be it real or imagined) hurts, threatens, or interferes with the balance, the natural response is fear. Tell the patient that fear is a sign of weakness and his ego will confirm by declaring, "Why yes, that would show vulnerability." So, he will suppress the fear and it seems to magically transform into anger. The approval-seeking mechanism jumps in and states, "Oh, but anger is socially unacceptable. I can't show that." The anger smolders, the sense of injury deepens, and a resentment begins.

At this point, you want to tell the patient the only way to clear this resentment is through assertiveness and confrontation, but this is an uncomfortable thought. He could lose the argument if the other party is a better debater, or yells louder, or walks away. Nope, too much at risk. So the resentment turns inward and becomes remorse. The remorse turns into self-pity. Self-pity sends him into depression, then into isolation, and isolation keeps him in ignorance. Ignorance causes errors in thinking, judgment and action, and these mistakes bring about fear, and the cycle starts again. This is just where we want him. The emotions stack up like the layers of an onion, with each round of nonsense serving as the foundation for the next and the entire cycle begins again.

See? Once you get proficient at this, you can take your patient all the way through the entire sequence in a matter of seconds (in terrestrial time) without the patient ever realizing what happened. For example, his spouse criticizes a minor point, or he is not called upon to speak in a meeting, and the patient goes straight into a sullen depression. In this way, each time around, the shadows are cast a little longer, a little darker, and the patient moves ever so slightly further out of reach of the Enemy.

There are only two things we must do: 1) maintain the extremes by alternately affirming the grandiose ego and the low self-esteem, and 2) quietly nudge the patient along the entire progression from fear to isolation. This keeps the truth away from the patient and the patient away from the truth.

Which truths? The truth that the balancing act is being performed on an impossible teeter-totter. The truth that the cycle is like a non-stop merry-go-round with no ring. The truth that other people are whirling along on their own absurd assumptions, so collisions are inevitable yet rarely intentional. And ultimately, the truth that he can get off the wild, spinning ride any time he wants. He only needs to ask for help from the Enemy, who is always right there quietly waiting to be asked. The very thought of that makes *me* dizzy and nauseous.

So if your patient actually starts the resentment inventory, convince him a mental one is adequate. If he insists on doing it in writing, and is working from the book, have him get all his information from the page with the example, and not from the instructions that are in the text. This is the same approach used when the patient is confronted with mechanical things which have "some assembly required." As he fumbles trying to unfold the oversized instruction sheet, you are telling him, "This is easy, you already know how to do this." If anyone else is watching—such as a child, a spouse, friend, or even the dog—your patient's ego will eagerly agree with you, pushing the poor fellow off into the deep end. Meanwhile he rationalizes it for you, thinking he jumped in voluntarily.

The reason to limit his use of the book is the section that asks him to look at his part, his mistakes. We want him satisfied with a simple list of dirty, rotten, filthy, nasty things he has done. It makes for better guilt if he stops here. Otherwise he could discover it was distorted thinking followed by errors in judgments that lead to his regrettable actions. From here he might begin to see our part in it. And this must be prevented.

The Enemy boasts of breeding these humans for humility, but *we* are the real experts at humility. We want our work to go completely unnoticed. We are content to be in the background, tending to our little gardens, drawing no attention whatsoever to ourselves. But do we get any credit for this? No. None at all. The Enemy would have our patients drag us into the open and publicly accuse us of fraud and deception. They would paint us as vile, grotesque little creatures who open up huge holes in the earth to swallow up the humans. That's totally wrong! Well, mostly wrong, anyway. We are simple masons building a wall, brick by brick, from whatever materials we can scavenge, to protect our patients from the harsh elements and brutal truths. And the Enemy would tear it all down, instantly vaporizing it into dust in a single, blinding flash of light, which is nothing more than a patient's awareness of the truth, and of Him.

You can see it is very important to minimize any advantage the Enemy attempts to gain. We must remain diligent. So, now, if your fellow is continuing with the step work, he may be at the fear inventory.

Oddly enough, fear is one of the Enemy's creations. It is designed into the very fabric of these humans. But we have made better use of it. We have taken His simple, practical idea and turned it into our most productive tool. The original application of fear was intended for a call to action as part of the "fight or flight response." Imagine an early caveman grubbing around for food, when suddenly something very hairy with lots of teeth jumps up from behind a rock and growls at him. This is where fear comes in. The human has to make a decision about a course of action. Either he is going to kill and eat this thing, or else he must outrun it so it does not kill and eat him. He makes his assessment of relative strength and endurance, he appraises the surrounding terrain for obstacles or advantages, checks his visual field for any makeshift weapons, calculates the odds, and then initiates the plan of action. Fear has now fulfilled its function. It is all is done in about one second. In terrestrial time that is very, very short.

Fear is a very useful survival instinct. There is nothing untoward or inherently evil about it. However, link it to the ego and you have some real potential. Take fear out of the present and its incredible power becomes clear. Since all action takes place in the "now," fear is completely out of its natural element once the imagination gets hold. One cannot take action in the future, so the fear keeps running. It gains momentum and size, blowing itself up completely out of proportion, and out of control.

Let's say your patient's boss offers some constructive criticism. From here you start to play "what if" with the patient. "What if the boss *really* doesn't like you? What if he fires you? No job, no money. What will you do then? Will your family leave you? You'll be abandoned, left all alone, homeless and broke. Then what will people think? That you are a worthless failure?" Your patient's natural fear instinct will give him the two fight-or-flight choices: punch out the boss or quit the job. Neither one is a particularly good option, and in most cases, the patient will search for other avenues. He may disguise his hostility as aloofness, or console himself with the petty theft of time or tools or supplies. He may speak badly about the boss and start to gossip, although he would be greatly insulted if you called it that.

Fear, in conjunction with the resentment cycle, can be easily maintained, because it often generates its own momentum. However, a fear all by itself is a very fragile thing. I had a patient convinced for years—even though he was well into his sobriety—that he was afraid of heights. While on vacation, he went on an excursion in the jungles of Central America, climbing and exploring a Mayan pyramid. As he was ascending a forty-foot vertical section on a rickety old ladder, I had him terrified—frozen in place. People above couldn't come down. People below couldn't come up. Oh, it was delightful. I was standing back enjoying the situation, admiring my handiwork when suddenly he realized he was not afraid of *heights*. He was only afraid of looking foolish or stupid if he fell. His self-image was that of a man always in control, and he did not want to spoil it by being a center of negative attention. He figured out all he had to do was keep a good grip, take one rung at a time, and there was virtually nothing to fear. Years of meticulous work were obliterated in an instant.

The key to minimizing the effectiveness of your patient's fear inventory is the same as other parts—limit his work to merely writing a list. Have him gloss over the instructions about asking "why." If he does ask, make sure he asks only once. The automatic first response will almost always be an excuse. When a human asks "why?" four, five, or six times, digging deeper with each pass, chances are he will eventually uncover the truth. Here is how it went for my patient:

Why are you afraid of heights?
I'm afraid I'll fall.
Why are you afraid of falling?
I'm afraid I'll hurt myself and make a big scene.
Why is that a problem?
Because I'm supposed to be in control.

Why are you supposed to be in control?

Because I'm cool.

Why are you cool?

Because I'm supposed to be better than I am.

Why is that?

Because someone who was full of crap told me a long time ago that I wasn't good enough—I didn't know any better so I bought into it. That's why!

It is true?

No!

So are you afraid of heights?

No.

Then start climbing!

So you see, keep the fear list as superficial as possible. We would rather they merely itemize their fears, and if they must try to follow the instructions in the book, have them list only the simplest of reasons why they had the fear. Actually a rationalization on why they should hang on to them would be even better. As you know, fear is not a sin, but it is a good foundation for bad assumptions. A patient's assumptions are the first layer of bricks in a wall that we want to build very high.

Now about sex. If your man has been working on his inventory on a regular basis, let him know it's OK to take a break. A few days or a few weeks won't matter. He will gladly defer doing the writing called for by this part of the inventory. Since he's not writing, he probably should refrain from attending the meetings his sponsor goes to, because his sponsor would ask him how the work is coming. The delightful dilemma here is that it sets him up to have a resentment against his sponsor. If he writes about the resentment, he would have to read it to him during the Fifth Step, which is too fearful to consider. His only other choice is to not write about it, but then he will be hiding a secret from the sponsor. This is all very good. You can see where you are headed with this. Hopefully, the patient will not.

Sex is another of the instincts the Enemy gave to all the animals. It has a reputation for causing all sorts of difficulties for which we have been given credit, where none is due. That's fine, though. If the humans see the deed as the sin, it is better cover for our work.

Sex can only really be enjoyed in the present, in the "now." The Enemy made it that way. Perhaps He thought it would limit our access to it. It does limit it, but we are not really interested anyway, thank you. The sin is not so much in the act, but the degree to which the thoughts about the act distance a human from the Enemy and from other people. Thoughts in the future— as fantasy or fear or clandestine premeditation. Thoughts in the past—as guilt, remorse or shame. Such thoughts are about the self—the ego attempting to be in charge, in control of the external world, at whatever price.

In reality, most of the issues are not about sex at all, but about self-esteem, pride, ambition, security, and the like. Sex is merely the stage where these plots and subplots are played out. The curtain rises. Costumes, lights, script, actors, a director, then *action*! This time it will be different. This take will be flawless. This time it will turn out just the way he or she wants. After the show, the critic—the ego—moves in and mercilessly and unforgivingly tears the show to shreds, replaying each fumbled line and awkward move over and over again. Expectations on the other person or the fear of expectations from the other party begin to creep in. Approval, disappointment and rejection swirl in and out of the picture. The mind begins searching for the fix, the change in the script, the change of characters, so that next time will be perfect. And thus we play and replay the endless loop.

Concerning the inventory work, point to Step Five and ask, "Do you want to tell this stuff to somebody?" If your patient forges ahead anyway, have him inventory only his deeds. It can be superficial or in lurid detail. It doesn't matter, as long as he refrains from questioning his thinking or real motives. If he is normal, he will think his emotional reactions to things on his list are "guilt." Guilt is a noun, but most humans treat it as a verb. Guilt means they did or they did not, that's all. What they *feel* is shame, remorse, or fear—usually fear of getting found out. So, stick with guilt, the verb, as a great way to distance the patient from the Enemy.

It should not be difficult to sense when your patient is stalling on doing his sex inventory. You need to be ready to kick the pencil out of his hand the moment he hesitates. If he has done anything regarded as illegal, immoral, spent a summer on a farm with small animals, or has engaged in self-entertainment with inanimate objects, he will certainly flinch at the thought of putting pen to paper. He may balk at conflicting feelings about masturbation. Don't let him know that if the Enemy had a hands-off policy, the organ would be somewhere in the middle of his back, or else his arms would be much, much shorter. If your patient has even remotely considered the question of sexual orientation, keep this kind of thing in the front of his mind, but completely off the paper.

When he stops writing for even a moment, suggest he is thirsty or hungry. Have him walk past an open window and get distracted by something he sees in the view outside. Point out the television and ask him, "Isn't there something good on?" If this TV ploy works for your patient, restrict him to watching news, sports or mindless comedy. Stay away from documentaries on animal mating habits as it might remind him of his neglected inventory. Have him pass on the romantic dramas, too, as they are just fictionalized human versions of what goes on in the nature films.

If he skips over the "sane and sound ideal" part of the inventory instructions, as many of them do, so much the better. It requires prayer, and there is little we can do to muddle up even a bad prayer if it is said in earnest. If he sees the part about "mold our ideals," help him fix an unrealistic or unattainable one. Pick anything from current fashion, advertising, films, or TV. In one of my finer moments I almost had one middle-aged, male patient convinced that since he imagined he had twice the libido of his forty-year-old wife, he ought to be able to trade her in for two twenty-year olds.

As I have stated before, the best outcome would be that he does not even start an inventory. Next best is that he not complete it. So if you can get him to stall, you can get him to stop. Once he has stopped, discourage him from resuming the work. The outside things in his life will go OK for a few days. Tell him, "Maybe you don't really need this A.A. deal after all." Once he has missed a few meetings, he can miss a few more and so on, until you are free of the A.A. problem.

The slow, steady approach, my friend. Easy does it.

Your friend,
Glumlot

Letter Thirteen

Dear Twigmold,

So, your patient has now finished his inventory and is considering Step Five. See if you can get him to associate it with Catholic confession. If you have been following the standard protocols you learned back in Training College, then he should hold a pretty dim view of that practice. A thin veneer of haughty disdain is more than enough to insulate him from the Enemy on this front.

If you've done your homework, your fellow will still have his ultimate secret stashed far away, off in the shadows. The one you've been telling him shall never see the light of day. It is too horrible, or too humiliating, or too whatever for him to admit to anyone. I like the drama of the phrase, "Take it with you to the grave." Make it attractive with images of a green, serene, hilltop cemetery with tall, majestic shade trees gently swaying to the rhythm of a warm, strong, early summer breeze. Rustic wooden benches stand patiently idle along winding, narrow stone paths, all under a clear blue sky. In rhythm with the wind, small yellow flowers bow and nod their heads towards a simple, gray granite stone with his name and the simple epitaph, "Nobody Found Out."

Even if he wrote *the* secret down as part of his inventory, I trust you will continue to advise him it would be in his best interests to casually skip over it as he reads his inventory to his sponsor. Who's to know? Remind him of the parts of Chapter Five, which they read at the all the meetings, that say "progress, not perfection" and "we are not saints." Reassure him that he's done a fine job as it is, and there is no point in being obsessive about his inventory. Enemy agents are always telling him "moderation in all things." Well, you ought to agree, at least as it applies to Step Five. Give him a message of moderation and he will assume it's from the Enemy!

If you take care of these preliminaries, under most normal circumstances, there would be very little to be concerned about. However, I have checked the dossier of your man's sponsor, and it looks pretty bleak. He is reputed to have a very drastic approach to this step. According to the file, his method is based on the absurd premise that the Enemy, being non-corporeal, has no ears so must borrow those of a human through which to hear the reading of the inventory! Isn't that ludicrous? If he left it alone at this bizarre point, it would be nothing more than amusingly strange. But he goes on to invoke a simple prayer at the beginning of the session, inviting the Enemy to join them. Of course, the Enemy, who is all forgiving, overlooks the ridiculous business about the ears, and actually shows up. I have absolutely no idea what happens after that because the view is totally obliterated by the asphyxiating cloud of His presence.

Why does the Enemy pretend to place such a premium on truth, and then puts up with that illogical nonsense about His not having ears? His tolerance of such foolishness only reinforces it. You can see why there is widespread skepticism about the Enemy's proclaimed meritorious motives. I think it is blatant propaganda. It is so obviously duplicitous that the humans must really be very naive or stupid to not see through it. However, naive and stupid work in our favor too, so maybe that's just another element in the art of war. I don't know.

As far as the reading assignment the sponsor gave your patient, about the best you can do is apply your standard distraction methods. The chapter is entitled "Into Action," so have your patient gloss over it as just a title, and not see it as part of the instructions. Better he should proceed "Into Thinking."

The original author of the book must have been very refreshed and focused when he wrote this chapter. Our tempter had kept him up quite late the night before on an obsessive writing binge, but, despite this, the man woke up invigorated and recharged. Obviously this was another case of the Enemy being immediately at the ready to undo our work. So, we must likewise always be prepared to respond in kind.

The author wrote about getting a "new attitude." As your patient reads this section, don't let him stop to ask what the words really mean. Let him assume he knows. Most humans figure that attitude refers to thinking, or snobbishness as in, "She has an attitude." The real essence of the word is an orientation toward action, based on the assumption of the validity of one's beliefs.

For example, if a patient runs around thinking he is supremely important and responsible for everything because he knows best, he will alienate most people around him. They withdraw or retaliate as the case may be and the man is now the owner of a first class, justified resentment that further isolates him. The opposite tack works just as well. A patient's self-loathing and sense of worthlessness are readily reinforced by the hard-charging first type. The result is the same: we have taken him another step down the slippery slope.

It all starts with a subtle suggestion to the ego. The ego will buy into the flimsiest of assumptions if it corroborates the ego's assertion of the central and supreme position. Conversely, it will dismiss anything that is of no use in supporting this delusion. So we carefully feed this creature—the ego—what it wants to hear, and it does our bidding for us. This is the most fundamental reason we do not reveal ourselves. We don't have to. A human can be easily led to think our suggestions emanate from somewhere deep within himself. The ego is always ready, able, and willing to assume responsibility for everything, and we make the most of this absurdity. When the patient chooses to act on our urging, with the desired dire results, he also takes on full ownership of all the guilt, remorse, and shame. Isn't this grand? But this is all very basic stuff.

Back to the Big Book. When your man reads of discovering the obstacles in his path, don't let him ponder about "what path?" or the fact that you have restricted his list to a meaningless enumeration of disgusting deeds. The obstacles (the ego's assumptions) are your real trophies. The things that block him are impediments to your patient only if he chooses to reverse his direction. You have him headed toward the shadows and the road ahead is clear. Tell him our path is the easier, softer way. Why, it's even all downhill from here. (Albeit a long, long way down.) If he turns around and faces the light, he will see the way scattered with the wreckage of his past—a mess *he* would have to clean up in order to get past it. It can only be removed by completely abandoning everything you have taught him, and tossing out all his assumptions about what is important (him and his desires), his priorities (him and his desires), and his relationship with other people (them and their desires). To top it all off, he would have to share this in detail with another person in Step Five. No, I think your patient should be happy to limit this step to admitting the exact "details" of his wrongs, not the "exact nature" as the written step indicates.

You are quite fortunate to have a patient in the age of television. We have not yet fully eliminated reading but the prospects seem to be improving daily. Even now, chances are slim that your patient would have read the British writer who penned, "If you don't tell the truth about yourself you cannot tell it about other people."[8] That's precisely our whole idea. We want him ignorant of the truth and in a state of utter complacency. This sets him up for poor participation in all his relationships, which further isolates him.

You also need to watch out for several other little traps the Enemy may try. One is the "anything else?" question from the sponsor. It is intended to dislodge *the* secret. The other is the "about-face," which can occur just after the patient walks out the door. I lost an otherwise well prepared patient at the very last second by assuming I had won and began relaxing to savor my victory. I didn't notice that the Enemy agents were still working very hard to exhume the ugly little piece of business I had helped the patient keep hidden away. Before the patient was half-way to his car, they got him to turn around, go back and knock on the door. In a panic, I let loose with all the noise I could muster, but was still drowned out by that ghastly melodious and malodorous air. The door opened and patient said, "There is one more thing. May I come in?"

In order that you do not make this same mistake, I recommend being relentless at this phase. Keep at it with your patient until he is in his car and far enough down the street to encounter another driver. Too fast, too slow, no blinkers, too old, too young, music he does not like being played much too loudly, anything will do.

Finally, not all sponsors will emphasize the very last part of the step that instructs the patient to go home and "...be quiet for an hour." In most cases you ought to be able to have your man take it as "...*be* for an hour." If you are doing your job, just *getting* quiet can take up most of that time. Any period of real mental silence—other than a blackout or unconsciousness—gives the Enemy a decided advantage. So as always, noise is the elevator music in the long descent to Hell.

Your friend,
Glumlot

P.S. See if you can coordinate with Grimsnore to assure the sponsor is very tired when it comes time to hear your patient's Fifth Step. With a little luck, the sponsor might fall asleep during the reading and your man will be deeply insulted that his grand work of gut-wrenching truth is just another cure for insomnia.

Letter Fourteen

Dear Twigmold,

I was puzzled by the statement in your letter about the "good news" of having both tears and laughter in your patient's Fifth Step. If the tears were about self-pity, that's fine. If they were tears of joy, that's not good. If the laughter was out of awkward shame and self-conscious embarrassment, this would be excellent. If it was laughter at the sudden sense of freedom from the release of old ideas—that's very bad. Worst of all would be if the patient was laughing at you. For some reason, a human will break into riotous laughter at the sight of the Enemy blowing apart years and years of our persistent, painstaking work. The human emotions overflow and start a chain reaction that inescapably spirals in toward the very present moment, and all the Enemy's secret hiding places therein. Such laughter is so disgusting it almost as vile as music.

Did you know that human emotions may follow very precise physical laws? One particular law that comes to mind is the eighteenth century French chemist Lavoisier's "conservation of matter." It is supposedly an energy-to-matter, matter-to-energy thing, which is peculiar to the physical plane, so I don't claim to fully understand it. But, assume for the moment that emotions are like energy. Once an emotion has started, by thought or whatever, it must manifest itself to an equal degree in some form, physical or otherwise. If it does not find its primary target, an outward action such as laughter or tears, it will turn inward to the physical body. There it becomes a nervous twitch, a throbbing headache, or chronic indigestion.

Now, from our perspective, the emotions always move in one of two directions: toward the light or toward the dark, toward the Enemy or toward Our Father Below. That leads me to a hypothesis: when an emotion is under Enemy influence, its principle objective could be love, health, creativity, action for the benefit of others, or some such uselessness. What *we* try to do is pull it off course, and move it into the darkness. We apply our skills to redirect the momentum toward pain or fatigue—real or imagined. We transform the energy of these errant emotions into long-suffering, undiagnosable, malingering maladies without hope of treatment or relief.

Since the assumptions are the springboard of thought, and thought the driver of emotions, our effort at twisting the truth is really an endeavor to re-aim and re-focus this energy by control of the starting point—the patient's basic attitudes. A thought launched from false assumptions will invariably go awry, creating emotions for which there is no "real" target. Like a misfired missile that falls back to earth unleashing merciless destruction on unwary victims, these misconceived emotions boomerang to burrow deep under the skin of the patient. Only to flower and bloom in our sheltered little gardens as bouquets of endless suffering from perceived injustices of unthinkable proportions, debilitating pain, unrelenting sorrow—we could increase the list ad infinitum.

So it makes sense that our most effective strategy is not to fight the Enemy head on, but to slowly turn the patient away from the light. Start to replace "real" with "normal." Gradually suck the color out of everything until all is gray. All other hues become gaudy and garish. The assumptions of expectations are replaced with the certainty of disappointment. The emotional misfires become so tedious, that it would be better to feel nothing at all. Can't you just picture it? Plodding along stoop-shouldered, head down, dead to the world, and all alone. A patient like this is your best bet. Not very dramatic, to be sure, but it is reliable. You can be quite optimistic about him making it to the end of our road. By time he looks up, sees the Gates of Hell and realizes where you've delivered him, it's already over!

I am sorry if all of this has sounded like a commercial for the slow and steady approach, but my experience is that it works. The Enemy is known for His ostentatious methods (which He calls miracles) that are, regrettably, quite effective. But don't forget that the Enemy also relies primarily on the slow and steady procedure. It is used far more frequently than even most humans imagine. It can be just as successful as

His more drastic and dramatic method. I suspect there is no qualitative difference between the two, just that one takes place over a much shorter period of time, which makes it more noticeable.

Now, I think we offer a better deal. We do not require our patients to sit through any promotional meetings where baskets are passed. There are no recruitment drives. There is no mandatory reading, no chastity, no dress code, no prayers, no hymns, no rules of conduct, no memorized recitations, no chanting, no Steps to work, and—best of all—no sobriety.

But the Enemy? The Enemy separates Himself, by means of the human ego, and then wants to be invited to dwell inside the patient. It is a conspicuously invasive proposition. It starts from a point of exclusion. Be we are *inclusive*. We wish the humans inside us. We offer our patients the chance to be "part of"—part of something larger than themselves, but without any compromise of the ego required. The Enemy insists they let go of old, comfortable ideas so He can conquer from within. We build up personalized, dedicated fortifications to protect everything the patient already is, thinks he his, pretends to be, or wishes he was. The Enemy asks for total surrender. We offer shelter. The Enemy demands sacrifice every step of the way. We ask for nothing at all. (At least not until the very end.) The Enemy says they should pray each day for their meager allotment of bread; that they should thirst for what He offers. We gladly fatten them up to have a place of ultimate honor on a splendid banquet table where they will be appreciated and savored. The Enemy's proposition has all sorts of strings attached. There are conditions to be met moment by moment throughout the patient's daily life, for all of their human existence. For what? In exchange for a promise of some vague, ethereal benefit. We ask for no up-front deposit, we charge no interest, and all payments are deferred. Granted, the final payment is *very* final, and the no-return policy is strictly enforced.

One of the nebulous promises of sobriety comes from a story in the book about a fellow and how the Enemy "...had done for him what he could not do for himself." This phrase is occasionally quoted in meetings, but is rarely discussed in any meaningful detail. However, I believe it does warrant *our* examination and study. First, we should consider what are the things he cannot do for himself?

Can your man stay away from the next drink? Given his physiological and mental predisposition, the answer is almost certainly that he cannot. But you can bury this truth by suggesting that since *he* goes to meetings, and *he* reads the book, and *he* does the commitments, then *he* is obviously the one doing all the work, so *he* ought to be the one to get the credit for his sobriety. Your man has probably heard and maybe even seen that A.A. members who quit doing those things often get drunk. So therefore, his actions must be directly and solely responsible for the maintenance of his abstinence.

Can he control the results and outcomes of his actions? No, he cannot. These are totally out of his hands. (They are out of ours also, but I don't want to get started on that.) Can he make other people feel or think in any certain way? Again, no. His actions may influence others, but it does not mandate any particular train of thought or emotional response. But let him believe that he really does have this ability. You can set this up by pointing out that other people often seem to be the cause of his feelings. Then it would logically follow that he can do likewise with them.

So then, what are the things he *can* do? He can make choices and take action. That's pretty much it. Decide and act. Think and move. Ponder and perform. When I stop to think about it, it seems absurd that the Enemy makes such a fuss over these animals when that is all they can do. Really, it seems almost funny. I don't mean humorously funny. Of course not. I am well aware that any degree levity is unacceptable decorum for tempters. What I meant is that is seems so senseless.

Anyway, the matter of making choices and taking action is the essence of the "will and lives" mentioned in Step Three. The humans have two choices: they can take direction from the Enemy, or from us. Their Big Book refers incessantly to this business of asking for and receiving directions. It talks about strength and direction, care and direction, power and direction, purpose and direction, inspiration and direction. It goes on and on. Why all the repetition? I think it is pretty clear that the humans don't like taking direction and being told what to do. This is especially true with the alcoholics. So we have the advantage when we enlist the ego as the eager recipient of our suggestions.

Now, as for those things the patient *can* do for himself, he should "let go" and relegate all of them to the Enemy. For example, tell him that his next promotion at work is entirely up to this mysterious, heavenly non-entity. Your man has nothing whatsoever to do with it. He is totally powerless and so it logically follows that there is no need for any effort, hard work, well-timed visibility, or political savvy. Say that any prospect of improved relationships with his family is wholly within the purview of some remote and obscure deity, so the patient needn't become a better listener, or try to be pleasant, or remember to pick up his dirty socks. With these techniques, you can have him substitute fatalism for faith, and disguise sloth as merely being passive.

If he is not receptive to this approach, take him to the extreme opposite point, where he fashions himself as the ultimate, free-thinking and independent man, aloof and above everyone, including the Enemy. Would he take direction from some external source? Well, of course—if it was needed. Since he is not a fool, he would be the first to accept help, but he does not need any help, and besides, it wouldn't be necessary for a man of his intellect and stature. You should hope you get a patient like this. These are the easy ones.

Of course, no matter what method you use, you will want to maintain your anonymity. Human literature most often speaks of the "Devil" as a singular entity. It usually refers to Our Father Below and the artistic renderings always seem to include the absurd, sinister red attire. As distasteful as it seems, do not dispute this image should it arise. Have your man think there is just the one devil, very distant and quite external. Let him have no clue as to our real numbers, nor that he has *you*—his very own personal tempter who will be at his side to guide him and protect him until his dying day. Finally, you may find that some humans expound the ridiculous notion that "...man created the Devil in his own image."[9] I trust you can let such rubbish pass without comment. No matter how offensive it may be, each untruth held by your patient is another stone in the wall you are building around him. As we have no other source of raw materials, you must make do with what is available.

——Glumlot

Letter Fifteen

Dear Twigmold,

Since you asked for input on Step Six, I can tell you the good news is that the instructions are deceptively simple. The average A.A. member who has reached this point will notice the fog is lifting enough to where the intellectual functions are returning, often with a vengeance. Let him spin his wheels trying to "understand" the program or "figure it out." This delaying tactic will give you plenty of time to implement your diversionary strategies. The bad news is that the step is really very simple, and about the only hope you have is to offer distraction.

The operative word for Step Six is willingness. It is crucial to render this step as ineffective as possible, because the next step is a blatant prayer. There things you can do which might mitigate or even neutralize a prayer, but if you can undermine the willingness that precedes it, you will be much better off.

It is important then to understand the roll willingness plays. Theoretically there are an infinite number of steps between thought and action. I find there are roughly seven stages: experience, assumption, belief, thought, willingness, faith, and action. However, not all human mental processes go through all seven.

For example, habit will skip from assumption directly to action with no intermediate stops. Generally, we prefer minimizing most actions because they always occur in the present, and there is no sense letting our patients linger in Enemy territory.

The first stage, the foundation of the process, is the sum total of the patient's experiences. These usually originate from external sources: parents, teachers, the media, superstition, current events, interactions with other people, and so forth. These are the basis for the second stage—assumptions. I think I wrote about these in one of my earlier letters. This is where the ego gets plugged in, where a patient's version of the truth is established, and where we can do our best damage. The assumptions lead to number three, belief. Belief rarely questions, and the act of believing reinforces the assumptions. Stage four is the conscious thought, the cognitive process, the conjecturing, the mulling over of things. This is a great place to hold your patient, because the echoes and feedback are so strong and so persistent that the noise level can multiply very rapidly. And noise is good. If we can stop the process here, then it will not lead to action. Stage five is willingness. The thought has now emerged. Willingness is where the momentum begins. It is a commitment to empower the thought toward action. The sixth stage is faith—faith that the action will produce the desired result or at least an acceptable one.

The last stage is action, and action can go in four

different directions. It can proceed out toward others, it can move inwards—toward physical or emotional self-interests, or it can loop back into more thinking. An extremely disastrous application of this third direction (the loop) is where the thinking is used in self-searching to become new experience that rearranges the assumptions. Clearly, this is to be immediately short-circuited if encountered. The fourth and final direction action can take is no action at all. This is not the paradox it would seem. The act of not acting is a matter of willful choice, an act of volition. It does not matter if procrastination is motivated by fear or sloth, it is still a conscious decision based on experiences, assumptions, beliefs, and so forth. As one very clever human, whom we have thus far been able to keep in relative obscurity, once said, "There is no such thing as inaction."[10]

Let's take a case through the entire scenario. My patient has enjoyed the *experience* of eating chocolate ice cream in the past, so he *assumes* that he still likes it. Since nothing seems to have happened to change it, he *believes* he would still like it. He *thinks* about having some. He has the time, the money, a way to get to the ice cream shop, and confidence that it won't spoil his dinner. He is *willing* to get up out of his chair and go. He has *faith* that the store is still there, is presently open, and they have his favorite flavor in stock. Up to this point he has not moved a muscle. He may have begun to salivate, but that's an involuntary physical response and outside the scope of this discussion.

Finally, my fellow takes *action*. He gets up, grabs his hat, his car keys, and goes to indulge his gluttony.

In a more practical example, a patient's young child comes into the living room, steps square in front of the TV, and asks, "Daddy, can you take me to get ice cream?" The man's *experience* is that he enjoys watching an uninterrupted sporting event on television. He *assumes* his time is his own and *believes* he deserves to spend it as he chooses. He *thinks* about abandoning the game, then considers abandoning the child instead. He is *willing* to risk alienating his child and has *faith* the youngster won't go crying to the mother, so he takes *action*, saying to the kid, "Not now, Daddy is busy." Resentment, guilt, and remorse may follow and another brick is laid in place.

As it applies to Step Six in the A.A. program, the willingness is based on the premise that most of the groundwork has already taken place. If you have been persistent so far, the ground is not very solid. The patient may have had the experience of having the obsession to drink removed, but will have trouble seeing how that relates to his present challenge. He may assume there is a God, but will also see Him as external, distant, and arbitrary. He believes the program works, or seems to work, or parts of it work, but he also believes that nothing is ever one-hundred percent reliable. His thoughts about having his defects removed will range from mild approval on some to screaming resistance on others. What will replace them? What if nothing replaces them? What will become of him? Who will he be?

It would be virtually impossible for a patient to get from this point of doubt and fear, to having the kind of complete willingness required to have his defects of character excised and removed. Without willingness he could not move on to having faith—the faith that the Enemy could or would remove the defects. Without faith, there is very little likelihood of meaningful action.

Our traditional and standard techniques are the ones to employ. Twisting the truth in this case is making sure the patient thinks the "defects" are his actions or the (direct or indirect) results of his actions. Don't let him know that what *would* be removed are the faulty assumptions that underlie his actions; the beliefs his ego holds so dear; the feelings that have become so predictable and comfortable. It is not his anger that would be removed. It would be the ever-present presumption of superiority or inferiority that allows him to feel justified in his anger; the delusion that things are always supposed to go his way; and the illusion that everything going on around him happens *because* he is the center of things.

You can obscure Step Six by pointing out the instructions are only one paragraph long and telling him, "Hey, there is nothing to do here." I had a patient who actually read the book, and found the implied prayer on willingness in Step Six. I used a little bit of carefully planted noise to interfere with his perception of the words. Where it says, "We ask God to help us be willing," I was able to get my patient to retain it as "...help us *to* be willing." By adding this one word ("to"), it converted the phrase to an infinitive, changing it grammatically into the future tense. This reduced it to a mere possibility, thus taking it entirely out of the present and clear of harm's way.

Finally, if at all possible, divert him from doing the step at all. Is he going to mixed meetings? Are there any females he considers attractive? If so, suggest that having his defects removed is akin to what they do to some male farm animals. Certainly he would want to permanently postpone such a brutal and barbarous surgical procedure. How could he ever be ready to have all his natural desires removed? Especially that one. Ask him, "Is this what they meant by *going to any length?*"

Your friend,
Glumlot

Letter Sixteen

Dear Twigmold,

I think it is important to address an issue you seemed to be implying in a round-about way with some of your remarks. You are well aware that I have worked with these humans for quite some time. It is inevitable that I would come across a few good ideas here and there. Yes, I admit that I sometime read over my patient's shoulder. I know there are those in the deep dominion who frown upon such activity, but I am certain they mean reading for enjoyment or, Hell forbid, for enlightenment. I regard what I do as the clandestine gathering of intelligence data, and I happen to believe that I am a pretty good spy.

Please understand that as part of my service to our great cause, I have been trying to uncover the Enemy's strategies as documented in the human literature. So please do not be paranoid when I share my findings with you. On the other hand, you are probably wise to avoid discussing the matter in any detail with anyone else in the Lowerarchy. There are the closed-minded types who have not spent much time in the field and don't know what we are up against. They seem to think their job is to make sure we are doing ours. (And the humans think *their* bureaucracies are Hell!)

Let me give you an example of the kind of material I find in the books and writings and why I think it is valuable. A skilled human negotiator and career statesman once said, "The absence of alternatives clears the mind marvelously."[11] From this I learned that I must do more than just distract my patient; I must be planning the next distraction. More importantly, I understand why it is imperative that I remain diligently one step ahead of the Enemy agents. Where they would restrict choices, I need to have an endless array of selections to offer if I am going to be successful.

This leads me to my next point: I really like your idea of finding a hobby for your patient. I also think it is very good timing, given where he is in his work on the Steps. "Let's see, should I pray for the removal of character defects or shall I finish yesterday's crossword puzzle?"

Ideally you want to find activities that are self-absorbing. Look for ones with desirable qualities, like a potential for obsessive behavior or an exposure to drinking. Does he like to gamble? Is there a bowling team at work? Does he still hear from his Saturday softball buddies? I personally think golf has been our greatest contribution. It consumes time, attention, money, and marriages. If your patient has any perfectionist in him, it will provide him endless frustration on the fairways as well as at home. He will forget all about A.A. in no time at all.

Have you suggested that he deserves a reward for

a shortage of
greed, envy,
victorious in t
the losers bec
not let your p
his education
front, payin
following inst
make learnir
would do any
pride, ambiti

Other hot
This affords
rewards. Sin
Enemy, you
Painting or d
of ability. If
obscene or vu

Music is e
any talent, o
usually suffi
associated w
style offends
and obscure
music requir
You can eve
motive is s
lustful inter
choir is us

his sobriety? Does he secretly want a new car, a motorcycle, or a boat? An impulse purchase of this magnitude, done without the spouse's approval, would do wonders. Plus, the short-term thrill of the acquisition will wear off just as the payments start, leaving him worse off than when he started. Then ask, "If you don't feel better in sobriety, why bother?"

Exercise is good as long as it is done to excess. Have him motivated by pride in his physical appearance or to be attractive to women and impress other men. (Or vice versa if that is the case.) If a patient is already in a relationship or has a family, his exercise regimen should take time away from those commitments so as to cause bitterness and suspicion at home.

If your patient is not physically athletic, then television sports are your best bet. The more sedentary he becomes, the more you can whittle away at his diet and health, which will make him all the more sluggish. Soon he will be both physically and mentally immobile. A home computer can be used to nearly the same effect, but with more potential for economic drain from the family savings.

If he is more the outdoorsy, puttering type, then yard work and gardening are good. Suggest he ought to have the greenest lawn, the best roses, the fewest weeds, the most tools—whatever. Just remember, all those growing and flowering things are the Enemy's handiwork. If your patient begins to bond with the "simple delights" of his garden and appreciates it for

the Enemy's
quickly sugge
that he ough
with his time

Generally
is not workal
options for
depending or
caring and g
the motivati
in a relation
then you ha
resentment.

If your p
the youngste
It takes only
an obsessed
degree of im
children, th
be the team
than any of
kid will not
the games,
will be easy
his A.A. me

Going l
newly sobe
very stron
institution:

However, I strongly urge you to avoid real "gospel music." We've not been able to determine exactly how, but it can evoke an onslaught of insurmountable Enemy influence on many patients. The only reliable exception to the general rule on music is going to the opera, which like getting drunk, is a sin that carries its own punishment.[12]

Did you know that most humans see themselves as being either male or female? I mean entirely one or the other. Isn't it remarkable how the trappings of the physical world influence their thinking? At any rate, for those who are predominantly female, there are some additional distractions you can use. There is the desire to resume a promising career relinquished to pursue motherhood. This can lead to a focus on promotions, money, and achieving equity with men in the workplace. With the right twist on things, this can be developed into militant feminism. In A.A. meetings you can use her indignation at the predominant use of the male-oriented terms in the Big Book to exempt herself from any of the directions or the Steps. You can even generate a mental block against God based solely upon popular use of the male subjective and objective pronouns in reference to the Enemy. (By the way, the human expression, "Hell hath no fury like a woman scorned,"[13] is never to be taken to have any implication or reference to the gender of Our Father Below, and I would never even repeat any rumors to that effect. Not unless I had all my affairs in order first.)

Now that your patient feels healthy and is working a program, a good distraction would be a focus on the spouse's faults. See if you can't help your patient develop an obsession to "fix" him or her. The same idea can be used as justification for re-establishing bonds with lost and dysfunctional family members. Because of his own recovery, the patient will feel superior, and therefore entitled to control their lives and to direct them to the appropriate recovery program. Of course, this will cause all sorts of problems, conflicts, ill-will and resentments.

The patient can become preoccupied with a child's schooling. He could become furious about the latest curriculum-du-jour that our friends in academia are always dreaming up. He can feel indignant and victimized by school administrators who have rapaciously adopted the latest fad as a means of securing tax dollars, which they greedily squander on themselves. Or, if you prefer, take it the other direction and you may have a meddling, self-promoting, do-gooder PTA president on your hands.

Just as a warning, I ought to caution you against allowing any hobbies that are truly and innocently pleasurable. They foster real contentment and open the patient to self-forgetting and even humility. This leaves him vulnerable to an intractable infection of serenity by the Enemy. This is another one of those putrid little "gifts" He likes to bestow on these creatures, His "children" as He calls them.

The key to successful distraction lies in what I call the Ego's Paradox. The ego wants everything to remain the same, yet is quickly bored with monotony. It wants to be in charge, yet does not want to be held responsible or accountable. It wants intimacy without vulnerability. It wants consistent variety, stable chaos, the virgin harlot, renowned anonymity and Godless sobriety.

There will always be resistance to full surrender by the ego, so always try to set aside part of the patient that he can keep for himself. Have it be his one final holdout against God. Teach him the mantra, "This is mine. This is mine," and eventually it will be yours. Eternally and internally yours.

Your friend,
Glumlot

Letter Seventeen

Dear Twigmold,

Thank you for your kind comments. I am glad to know that you have changed your mind and now see value and potential in the type of work and research I am doing. And you were quite right—I had intended to write to you about Step Seven but I got carried away. I shall try to address the matter forthwith.

Our tempter on the scene at the original writing of A.A.'s Big Book was able to reduce much of its clarity and focus, even though he was up against what seemed like impossible odds. However, the final publication was subject to input and approval by the two small A.A. groups in place at the time. After our disastrous experiences with other books with which the Enemy has been involved, we learned that there is nothing as effective to further our aims as a committee. The process of compromise, consensus, and democracy will water down practically anything.

In this fashion, our tempters working with the book's contributors got them to replace the "Humbly, on our knees, asked Him..." from the first draft of the Seventh Step, with "Humbly asked Him...." The whole idea of removing the phrase "on our knees," was to make the prayer less effective. One of my professors at the academy was always fond of pointing out that these humans are as much animal as they are spirit, and the posture of their prayers has a significant impact on its effect. However, I sometimes wonder if we had left it in its original form, with "on our knees" in it, would it scare off even more people than it does now?

If your patient is a determined book reader, bring his attention to the part that refers to the removal of defects which "stand in the way of his usefulness to others." Do you see the loophole here? You will find his ego an enthusiastic participant in restricting the application of this step to a limited definition of "usefulness." All you need to do, is get it started. Suggest that it does *not* include his disregard of his dog, impatience with his child, the self-righteous anger at stupid drivers, borrowed office supplies from work, his fantasies of infidelity, the outbursts of ill-temper with coworkers, etc. As he looks at a defect, frame your question along the line of, "This isn't in the way of being useful, is it? Good, let's move on, then."

Another approach is to make this step seem very deep and mysterious. Have him think and ponder then think some more. He'll drive himself crazy wondering why he doesn't "get it." Suggest something is wrong because he isn't seeing any lightning bolts or burning bushes. He may have heard the little witticisms passed around in some A.A. meetings that if you are having trouble with a particular step it is because you haven't properly completed the preceding one. I had a patient bouncing back and forth between Six and Seven for years waiting for a great flash of light.

Alternatively, you can have the step appear very simple—a one shot deal. The book says that after the prayer, the person has completed Step Seven. Have him read "completed" to mean he will never need to do this one again; he need not ever give it another thought; or ever revisit the prayer.

The best option, as I keep saying, is to have him not do the step at all. Have him looking back and forth between the future (doing the amends) and then the past (the filthy, rotten, nasty things he did). Play out a scene of him going back to some of those people and saying, "I stole from you" or "I lied" or "I was afraid and ran away." See where his fear and imagination take it from there.

If he has any outstanding business with the tax people or with the courts, you have some great material for building up a towering monolith of fear, which will cast a long, dark, and cold shadow. Surely you can find something from his inventory that you can use in this way.

If you look around at most meetings you will find more newcomers than long-timers. There are more who have started the Steps than have completed all twelve. Why is this? Because we let the Steps chase most people out for us. The unwilling are usually run off by the prospect of the surrender in Three, the inventory in Four, and the long talk in Five. The requirement for doing amends in Nine is the other great reason there are plenty of spare folding chairs and left over coffee. The idea of "facing the heat" can make an alcoholic mighty thirsty.

The second thing working in your favor is alcoholism itself. They are not cured. Many groups read a rather offensively mushy section of the book they call, "The Promises." However, there are other promises in the book, too. I like the one that says there will come a time when the alcoholic will have "no effective mental defense against the first drink." The only hope they have is intervention by the Enemy. It doesn't tell them that the Enemy must first get past the fortifications and defenses we have so carefully constructed.

So, have a chat with your patient about the good old days when he was drinking. Remind him it was not all doom and gloom. There were moments of riotously good fun. Ask him how many colorful slang expressions he can rattle off that mean "drunk." Things like soused, pickled, plastered, bombed, etc. When he is done, ask how many euphemisms there are for "sober." Odds are he will not be able to come up with any at all. Point out that this shows the relative importance between the two. Have him recall the rituals, the cracking of the ice tray and the crystal echoes of ice clinking in a glass, the beautifully rich, golden hues and smooth textured reflections in a tall scotch on a dark, mahogany bar. Bring up the physical memory of the wave of relaxing peacefulness that washes through after the first drink.

The one that surges up and through his body after the momentary nauseousness of the first swallow burns its way down his throat. As the ringing in the ears quiets down to a muted buzz, there is that familiar soft, warm glow welling up from deep inside. The shoulders drop and the muscles begin to relax.

Before this image fades, you want to make sure your patient is near somewhere that has liquor available, someplace where he feels either very comfortable or very ill at ease. Any big family get-together on the holidays will favor your odds of success, because you can capitalize on history, expectations, old behaviors, and confrontations. Slowly increase the volume and intensity of the mental background noise. Just as Enemy agents can drive us off with bright light, we can hold Them off with noise. If you have kept your patient out of step (no pun intended) and off his normal meeting schedule, or away from meetings entirely, the proper moment will come. That's a promise.

Some humans, especially non-drinkers, give *us* all the credit for getting our patients drunk. It is not like that at all. We suggest the first drink, but only the disease can hold the door open long enough for the idea to get in. No human in his right mind, who had an allergy such as this would ever drink again, but the illness somehow erases the memory or circumvents normal logic. We can knock on the door. It is the alcoholic who must answer. He must come alone if he is going to drink and once again set the cycle in motion. In some cases, the Enemy is at the gate with him. So you try again some other time. We can "Keep coming back," too!

Since your patient has been trying to find a spiritual experience, why not have him seek out some "distilled" spirits? If he does go out and drink, have him delight in the rebellion or wallow in remorse. Any reaction will do so long as it is extreme and unreal. Let him blame his failure on the program, "It didn't work." His pride will gladly support you when you tell him, "You can't go back now. What will they say?"

Don't get cocky, though. Try to keep your man out of any serious trouble. A severe incident with the family or the police could easily make him vulnerable to a move by the Enemy. Remember, They are working just as hard as you. In the morning after, they will be in full voice on a clear channel and ready to drag up everything he has ever heard in the A.A. meetings. Meanwhile, his stomach is dragging up the remnants of all your suggestions from the night before.

I do not want to create the impression that your primary purpose is to get your patient drunk. In some cases, the opposite could be true. Once a patient has a taste of A.A., a serious slip will probably drive him further either one way or the other. He could drink himself to death in short order, or he will return to the A.A. program and really try to practice it. The point is that you want to keep him off the spiritual path. I will not deny there is something very satisfying and rewarding in that moment when the patient realizes what you have done. The bottle pulls away from his lips, the liquid is sliding down his throat, the explosion is about to hit, when FLASH—he is suddenly aware he has *already* taken the first drink. It is too late. He has lost. You have won. Oh, the depth of despair and the hopeless resignation at that moment are very tempting, even for us.

However, let me remind you it is just a small taste, a bawdy tease, a cheap imitation of the real victory. Why settle for crumbs when there is a veritable feast awaiting you at Our Father's table when you finally bring a soul through the gates.

If you are very certain a drink will permanently turn your man our way and that it will cast an everlasting shadow over his A.A. experience, then go for it. But there are many other things you can use to block off the patient's contact with the Enemy. They may not be as dramatic or sinister, but they are far less risky. A patient can be quite sober—meaning free of the alcoholic addiction—and still be very much ours.

Your friend,
Glumlot

Letter Eighteen

Dear Twigmold,

A patient's work environment is an excellent area where you can make progress on a number of different levels. First of all, have him choose to keep his sobriety and affiliation with A.A. either a big secret, or broadcast it to anyone who will listen. The truth is most people won't care much one way the another. A few will be mildly supportive or at least courteous enough to try to appear that way. Some will be really turned off by his pulpit-pounding spiritualism. Others will be threatened by the very thought of abstinence from alcohol and will shun him out of concern for their own drinking. A few more will be similarly uncomfortable with anyone who actually practices a degree of self-examination and self-improvement.

The patient is probably still running around with a lot of raw nerve endings jangling about like exposed electrical wires. His attention span may not have yet recovered as much as the rest of him. He will seem way too flighty or too intense for most people. The patient may want the whole world to get the A.A. message. Tell him that he is obviously the chosen one to let them know, and he might as well start at his workplace. He may take on a smug superiority that pushes folks away.

130

He may place or receive too many A.A.-related phone-calls at work. Have him test his boss's tolerance by asking for unreasonable latitude in his work schedule to allow for morning meetings, noon meetings, leaving early, arriving late and so forth.

Your patient may have started to establish some boundaries. Like a child learning to walk, he is going to bump into things and hurt himself and maybe others. He has heard a great deal about being assertive from the people at the meetings. His sponsor may have given him permission to look out for himself. As the patient begins his first teetering steps with this new skill, you want to give him a quick shove so that he stumbles. Have him be unclear about the difference between assertive and aggressive. Tell him it means he doesn't have to take crap from anybody. Emphasize *anybody*. Have him try this on his boss or on an influential coworker. That should be fun to watch.

As your patient is still fairly new at sobriety, he can easily be persuaded to believe that because he has found the answer to his drinking problem, he now has the answers to all other problems. Have his creativity always focused on someone else's territory, so that he unintentionally offends and threatens his fellow workers in his desire to be "helpful." This will breed resentment from them, and he will be puzzled at their reactions and retaliations. Meanwhile, leave him only enough energy and interest to sustain no more than a mediocre performance at his own job.

He will very probably encounter resistance from a variety of people at work. Those who used to dominate and intimidate him will be quite displeased at his independence. The people who counted on him to draw all the negative attention away from themselves will be threatened by his new attitude.

Perhaps he has been under-employed for years and is now able to function at full capacity. His higher-ups (note: human bureaucracies are inverted) may see his potential, or they may not. They may care, and they may not. They may notice it and still be rather skeptical about the staying power of this new change. Suggest that he needs to make up for all those years lost to drinking. Tell him he must catch up on his career path, but can do so only by leaning hard on the people who hold the power. He has put the past behind him, so should they. He deserves that raise or promotion—now. Let him get self-righteous about it. Convert it into feelings of indignation, persecution, and self-pity if you can.

As you build up his desire for advancement, don't support it with rational motives like professional growth or providing financial stability for his family. Tap his lust for power, control, status, and prestige instead. You can even use revenge if the patient has a keen competitive sense coupled with a vulnerability to perceived injustice. As he looks around at others within the company who are getting promoted, have him notice only those who are of a different gender or race. Have him overlook those promotions that came about as the result of years of hard work, proactive problem solving, and positive, supportive relationships with superiors. If there is a rival coworker that your patient considers to be a conniving, manipulative, do-nothing, butt-kisser who has achieved greater recognition within the company, have the patient try to emulate those skills as his own means for promotion.

Another good play is the "career change." If one change is good (getting sober) then a lot of changes are even better. Have him throw away his years of experience for some ridiculous scheme or wild idea. Convince him that his new enterprise will solve all his other problems. If it requires substantial risk, debt, borrowing, mortgages, and eighteen-hour days, so much the better.

If he's not the entrepreneurial type, then he will be seeking work as an employee. If his plan includes mailing resumes, see to it that his curriculum vitae has at least one critical typographical error in it. Make the project seem so urgent that your patient feels hurried and he may even juxtapose digits in the phone numbers of his references. Then no prospective employer will be able to contact some of the people on his list. During interviews, have him preoccupied with thoughts like, "Should I tell them of my membership in A.A. or should I hide it? Would that be honest or not?" While he is busy thinking about that, he will give the impression of being distant, unfocused, and uninterested.

Have him oversell himself for a position for which he is not suitably qualified. With a little luck, he may get the assignment! Then you can work him up with fears of having to actually perform. Tell him he will be judged on what he *does*. They will have expectations; he will be monitored, reviewed, and evaluated. They will find him lacking and he will be exposed as a fraud. They will reject him and unceremoniously toss him out the door. Conjure up a mental picture of him airborne, arms and legs flailing about, an open briefcase spewing papers into the wind, and him—sprawling face-first onto a crowded sidewalk, teeth scattering in all directions like a spilled handful of dimes. Of course you will be there as he dusts himself off, to assure him it was all "their" fault.

I had one fellow who changed jobs about every year or so. He was quick to tell anyone who would listen about his incredible string of bad luck. He had worked for seven bosses in a row and every single one had been an idiot. Now, what are the odds of that?

Then again, you may be better off with your patient on the other side of the spectrum. If you have taught him to be risk averse, he will be afraid to even think about changing jobs. If he applies for one, they might decline his application. If he applies and gets an interview, they might reject him to his face. If he applies, interviews, and gets the job, he might screw up and fail some critical task and get fired. It is so simple to paint this kind of patient into a fearful, tight little corner.

If your man is of this type, you will want to watch for an exceptionally salient opportunity: the new boss. In most jobs, sooner or later, there will be a changing of the guard and your man will have to face reporting to a new and possibly unknown person. When this comes along, you want your patient stuck in the past. To every proposed modification of policy or procedure he should point out, "That's not the way we used to do things." He will quickly become a pariah, the odd man out. You will comfort him and agree that he is the innocent one, and they are all jerks.

There are other similar ways you can help your patient. For example, if he has learned about setting limits, have him limit the new technologies he his willing to learn. It is perfectly logical that with so many innovations coming so fast, he cannot possibly learn them all. So help him pass over those skills that would really benefit him in the future and have him choose to master only those that will soon be obsolete and quickly out of demand.

If he is at all self-righteous, maybe he could become a whistle-blower. Have him find and make a big deal out of discrepancies in the general manager's travel vouchers. If in sales, have him go overboard in his honesty, to the detriment of his employer, his own commissions and his career.

If he works in a service business, start to give him the idea that he really, really doesn't like people. He will savor his impatience and intolerance of them. If he works alone, and works best that way, have him think that he ought to have more interaction with the public, which can lead him to the same point of frustration.

When all else fails, get him caught up in one of the endless number of get-rich-quick schemes that our specialists in the Department of Avarice and Greed are always recycling.

Your friend,
Glumlot

Letter Nineteen

Dear Twigmold,

If I seem to have had a no-big-deal attitude with respect to your patient continuing to work the program, it is because Steps Eight and Nine are where we weed out the rest of the balkers. By this point in the steps, the patient will have built up some self-esteem, which the ego will automatically claim for itself. You should help the ego accept all the credit and glory for the progress thus far. This will bolster its own assumptions of supremacy.

As with the other steps, keep him away from the written instructions in the book. If you can't, don't worry about it too much, because most people gloss right over the willingness prayer in Step Eight and all four prayers in Step Nine.

It is all made easier because other aspects of the patient's life are improving. The situation at home is calmer, and things at work are more stable. So the implied urgency of the earlier steps is not as vividly apparent as before.

Don't let your patient forget that even the book says one can justify postponing amends, albeit under certain conditions. You just need to widen the parameters to include, "I don't feel like it."

It is not difficult to get your patient to procrastinate. Keep him in the future with thoughts of having to face the people he harmed. The automatic, physical response systems will let him feel all the horror, embarrassment and humiliation. Take him into the past by reliving each dreadful deed and he will suffer the agonizing shame again each time. If his list includes things he really enjoyed at the time, he will also be filled with ambivalence, confusion, and doubt.

Help him come up with reasons to not do a particular amend. "You can't repay your uncle the modest sum you owe him, because he would probably tell other relatives and then they would all want to be paid. Since you don't have enough to pay them all, it would be best to skip the amends to the uncle."

The other option I particularly like is the Ponzi amends, where he pads his expense account in order to get the cash to repay the uncle. Now he can't make the amends to his boss about his previous creativity on his expense reports because he is still doing the same old thing. Only now he is sober and can't blame the larcenous behavior on his drinking. Suggest to your man that since the boss always underpaid him anyway, this is just settling up an old score. So no amend is indicated. Now you have additional fears and resentment, with very little likelihood of your patient wanting to resolve it.

You see how simple it is? Make it complicated for the patient and it becomes simple for you. It doesn't matter if it is years of unpaid child-support payments or an overdue library book. Get him to put it off and any momentum he had will be converted into fear. Once you get him running from his fear, it always grows bigger.

Now, of course there are boundaries. Let's say your patient has a large unpaid debt with an ill-humored loanshark, or some other serious criminal type who would be inclined to permanently dispatch the patient solely in the interest of unpaid principle, or on the principle of unpaid interest. Despite the potential entertainment value of your patient's panic and terror, you ought to discourage him from making amends of this type, unless he has the entire amount in small, unmarked bills and is certain of walking away alive. Otherwise, you risk losing him to the Enemy who would look on the patient's foolish attempt at restitution with forgiveness. You will get much more mileage from day after tedious day, and night after sleepless night of exhaustion brought on by constant fear, worry, and anxiety over the matter.

If your man insists on doing some amends, let him do them poorly. One way is for him to take his new-found honesty and apply it with zealous self-righteous-ness. You can be comfortable that amends in this style will cause more harm than good. The patient will proudly think he has made admirable progress by bashing a stone loose from the wall you've built around him. Yet before the dust has settled, you will have replaced it with several new ones.

If your patient has any amends regarding old sexual behaviors, this is a wonderful time to fire the imagination. Have him try to anticipate the outcome. The result will almost certainly be a chronic fear of going "without" for the rest of his life, with good potential for all sorts of panicky and delightfully regrettable actions. This works especially well for male humans—for whom involuntary celibacy is generally a terrifying specter. Yet many tempters will spend years coaching their female patients to employ a similar form of abstinence as a control mechanism in relationships, meanwhile convincing them—get this—that it is just as satisfying. Isn't that classic? It leads to resentment and infidelity on one side, and spiritual pride and moral superiority on the other. In Hell, we get our share of virgins as well as the spitefully chaste, and the look of astonishment on their faces when they land at our door is priceless.

I will concede that our patients do get some real satisfaction out of doing proper amends. They liken it to unloading a heavy burden. So if your patient is determined to get started, have him do a few "easy" ones. He gets a taste of the positive sensation, and like anything that feels good, you can get your patient to want more and more. In his search for the rewarding experience, you can lead him straight away to the most complex amends, which he will most likely screw up. This causes more damage and he is left with the clear notion that he ought to stop making amends.

One of the key components to many amends is that grotesque contrivance of the Enemy, forgiveness. I don't mean the sarcastic, snobbish, self-engrandizing type that we encourage, but the syrupy and sincere, all-is-forgotten, from-the-heart kind. It will do untold damage to the protective structure you have been building up around your patient.

There are several ways to help your fellow revert to half-measures on the Ninth Step. One is to let him make the amends without forgiveness. A quick apology and a little money will take the heat off, which is enough to have the patient feel he has made progress. One human novelist, a woman who gave her tempter a lot of trouble, wrote, "It is easy to forgive others their mistakes; it takes more grit to forgive them for having witnessed our own."[15] If your patient starts to experiment in forgiveness with his amends, limit it to the first type (forgiving others their mistakes), and not the second kind (the witnessed errors). This second form can convert humiliation into real humility. Rest assured that during your career as a tempter, you will have very few patients gaining humility in this manner. This is because the Lowerarchy neither endorses nor practices forgiveness, and a tempter who is guilty of such negligence would be recalled in short order.

You will also want to avoid having your patient forgive himself. We would much rather have the patient condemn himself, preferably incessantly and without mercy. Our communications specialists have excelled in perpetuating the fallacy, to which most humans subscribe, that condemnation is one of the Enemy's primary missions. So when a patient unforgivingly damns himself, he is playing God. As long as a patient's ego has that ultimate leading role, it will not allow an understudy. If the patient's God (the ego) is judgmental, ruthless, fallible, and spiteful, there will be little incentive for spiritual growth.

I must admit, I have several fundamental problems with Steps Eight and Nine. The first is that it seems technically impossible for these Steps to have any effect at all. Let me tell you why. The grand contradiction is plainly evident in the A.A. literature. The book says the members cannot get over their drinking until they have cleaned up the past. Well, to the humans, the past is already long since over and the future is way off somewhere in the distance. It is illogical then, within terrestrial time, to clean up the past—because the past is inaccessible to humans. Further, how could future actions (not drinking) be dependent on an impossible modification of previous events?

However, as with all rules, there are exceptions. Two very small and very elite groups of humans are permitted to actually change the past: academic historians and political press agents. But the average A.A. member? Absolutely not. So this leads me to suspect that much of the Eighth Step willingness and Ninth Step amends process may be a hoax—a sham set up by the Enemy to divert our efforts and get us to squander our meager resources chasing meaningless nonsense.

Then there is the second problem. Steps Eight and Nine *appear* to actually work. Once a patient earnestly starts making amends, he begins to dismantle the walls we have built around him. As the walls crumble, more light comes in and he becomes even more susceptible to the Enemy's suggestions. Once torn down, you cannot rebuild the same walls again. You have to construct new ones, starting all over again from the very beginning. That is not a very inviting prospect.

Now, the Enemy wrote all the rules for the physical world, but does *He* adhere to them? No. The human literature is filled with evidence of *His* long record of crossing the line, and going way out of bounds for these loathsome, disgusting animals. At least one of the human philosophers got it right when he said, "The Prince of Darkness is a gentleman and whatever the God of Heaven and earth is, He can surely be no gentlemen for His menial services are needed in the dust of human trials."[14] The Enemy professes unwavering willingness to be constantly at a human's beckoning, to happily do for them what they are totally unable do for themselves. Wanting nothing in return but love. What utter nonsense.

It has never been a fair fight and it never will be, so why am I making a big deal out this? Maybe I am just envious that the Enemy can cut corners and gets to use all those dazzling special tricks. While our best weapon is everlasting and endless tedium, more of the same, nothing will ever change, hopeless, helpless, suffocating monotony. Not very flashy, but it works. It can turn a patient away from the Enemy and he may never look back. The best part is that we can often persuade a patient that what the Enemy calls "a few simple requirements" are really part of a never ending litany of outrageous and onerously oppressive demands—like confession, prayer, meditation, surrender, and honesty.

The Enemy would have our patient out in the open, stripped naked of all pretense, whereas *we* would have him heavily sheltered and insulated. And warm. Very, very warm. A properly prepared soul for Our Father's table has been slowly skewered and roasted over an eternal flame, heavily spiced with bitter resentment and peppered with fear. The Enemy claims to love the humans and wants to restore all to a pristine state, which is widely believed down here to be a ruse for precisely the same agenda we have for them. Only more like sushi.

Your friend,
Glumlot

Letter Twenty

Dear Twigmold,

All along, from the very start you have had many opportunities to distract, discourage, or divert your patient from "The Work." But it hasn't happened and now your patient is at Step Ten. This is not good news. The odds of your being able to draw him off now are very slim. This is because Step Ten is one of the easier steps to do. It says, "Continued to take personal inventory and when we were wrong promptly admitted it." At a basic level, many A.A. members start to put some of its tenets into practice long before they officially arrive at this step. The best you can do now to is to dilute its effectiveness and limit its application. Let's look at it piece by piece.

Where it says, "Continued to take personal inventory," have it be only the short, on-the-spot, mental assessments. Make sure it is not reduced to writing. The effect of paper and pen are far too permanent for us to allow. It incorporates three things: the thinking process, the physical act of writing, and the visual aspect of reading what is being written. With all of these occurring at once in terrestrial time, it implants the memory in three places—cognitive memory, muscle memory, and visual memory. It is practically impossible to dislodge facts when so affixed. If he does write, you will want to keep it very short and superficial. The real risk of additional inventory work is that his very first attempt, in Step Four, consisted mostly of the secrets he kept from other people. Subsequent inventories will reveal the secrets the patient has been keeping from himself.

Oh, and a warning: the patient may be invited to a "retreat" where serious reflection is encouraged and facilitated. Fortunately, these are usually held at churches or seminaries, so it would be wise to play up the perceived religious angle and make it seem like a front for evangelical recruitment.

On the "when we were wrong" part of the step, we can borrow one of the A.A.'s own slogans—Keep It Simple. Define "wrong" as being only the undesirable actions. Do not let it include the faulty assumptions, erroneous thinking and the misguided judgments that precede and justify the wrong action. If you can, narrow down the scope of "wrongs" to consist of only those actions that might have had witnesses. If nobody saw it, it was not really a "wrong."

See that the word "promptly" comes across sounding more like "eventually." Remind him of how the book thumpers (whom I always paint with words like "fundamental literalists") rant about the precise nature of the language in the book. So, by gosh, if they had meant "immediately" they would have written it as "immediately." You can also take the take opposite tack.

When the patient discovers he is in a position to apply this step, get him to hesitate. Then once the moment has passed, you say, "Oops, too late. It wouldn't be prompt anymore, so you might as well forget about it. No sense in living in the past." You need to do this very subtly, so that the patient doesn't have enough time to really consider what you've suggested. Some tempters use a very quiet whisper for this approach. Out of nowhere, a notion floats into the patient's mind and then disappears, darting back into the shadows before he can really see it. Like vanishing dreams on first awakening, or trying to reach for something floating in air—the act of trying to grab hold of it only pushes the thought further away.

As for the phrase, "admitted it," have him admit it only to himself, only in the most cursory manner, and only at an intellectual level. Chase away any idea that he has to *do* anything about it. Admit it? Sure. Change anything? No. With proper eroding of the foundations in a receptive patient, you can tell him he can do whatever he wants now; all he has to do is apologize if anyone gets bent out of shape about it.

If the patient seriously wants to try this step, have him apply it only to innocuous things. For example, a clerk gives him the wrong change—he gallantly returns the extra pennies. This works best if there is a line of other people behind him who all see his wonderful, selfless and humble sacrifice. Meanwhile, let him yell at his children without ever seeing a need to apologize.

The book implies it will be much more difficult to tempt a patient who is working Step Ten into resuming his drinking. The traditional methods will fail and your best efforts will seem to be ignored. Don't you hate it when that happens? Now, it is not terribly important whether he drinks again or not, for we have served up many a teetotaler at our feasts, but it does seem like it would be easier if he did. Maybe it's the principle of the thing. Where once we had a man so firmly in our grasp, to lose him to insipid sayings like, "Stay away from the first drink" is really irritating. You win some. You lose some. But I would rather lose in a fair fight to an admirable opponent, in a well-fought and courageous battle. There is dignity in that.

While it is generally true that our chances diminish rapidly as a patient starts on Step Ten, they do not totally vanish. It simply means we must work all the harder. As the patient gets more confident, you have more opportunities. Their Big Book is very clear on what we have to do. It says that the most an A.A. member can hope for is a daily reprieve and only if he keeps in fit spiritual condition. Your job is to keep him unfit and out of condition. Here the ego is on your side.

Congratulate him on *his* progress and suggest that he has now earned the right to lighten up on his meeting schedule. After all, he's heard the old-timers reciting the expression, "Easy does it." Maybe he should practice it in regard to the program. Besides, he could use the time for better things, right? Hasn't he been a little obsessive about all this lately? He's gone to speaker meetings, participation meetings, step-study meetings, book-study meetings, men's meetings, and mixed meetings. Then there is the step work, the service work, setting up tables, putting out the chairs, making coffee, drinking coffee, sweeping floors, taking down the tables, putting away the chairs, the meetings after the meetings with coffee and more coffee. Come on, he's been overdoing and he knows it. The Steps say if he is wrong, then he ought to admit it—promptly. So, let's promptly take a night off from those dreadful meetings. He owes it to himself.

You should also consider coming at this from an entirely different angle. Have him go to lots of meetings as a way of dodging other responsibilities or to avoid dealing with family issues. As long as it is causing damage that he is unwilling to fix, then maybe more meetings are OK. Take it far enough and perhaps the wife leaves. Have him blame it on A.A. rather than on himself. Wouldn't it be delightfully ironic for your patient to have a colossal resentment against A.A.?

You see, it is all a matter of making use of what you find. Don't waste your efforts trying to desperately invent new schemes to get your man off track. Be clever instead. Besides, it is better style to steal the very tools the Enemy left at the man's feet and use them against him. Turn kindness into meddling interference, humility into spinelessness, honesty into insensitivity, courage into foolishness, patience into stubbornness, and generosity into wastefulness. See what I mean?

Now, I did want to expand on the idea in your last letter about amplifying your patient's short-tempered tirades at other automobile drivers. There are some interesting dynamics and a good deal of potential here. It is a marvelous application of the concept I've mentioned before about having the patient retain some part of himself for his own exclusive use, free of the Enemy's influence, His principles and His rules; a corner of himself dedicated as a private playground for the ego.

While the Enemy gave the humans the creativity and inventiveness to produce mechanical transportation devices, we have been able to consistently establish the car, or truck, or whatever, as an unconscious symbol for the human ego. It is like a cocoon or an impenetrable outer shell. It is a power greater than themselves. Whenever they get in the car they become larger than life, invincible, they become the car. Is it any surprise that most of the vehicles look like animals? The act of being inside the car is so much like being inside themselves—inside the ego—that we can use this to assure their driving will correspond very closely to the self-image constructed from their key assumptions.

There are those who are immensely comfortable with themselves and will pay only as much attention to the outside world as is absolutely necessary. These are the sleepers. They never seem to notice that anyone else is around them. They drive slowly in the fast lane, never use their blinkers, and always leave their lights on high beam.

Next are people who are dreadfully uncomfortable in their own skin and are therefore terrified when in their cars. These paranoids drive even slower than the sleepers but never leave the slow lane. They will come to a complete stop on the freeways to let in merging traffic, especially big, heavy trucks and other slow drivers. If they have a high quotient for spiritual pride, we let them think they are doing it out of the goodness of their hearts. Meanwhile, they are helping us to infuriate and endanger other drivers. A win-win situation for us!

Finally there are those who are so overly concerned with themselves, they must counterbalance it by being overly concerned with what other people think. These are the true egocentrics. They are forever unable to resolve their impossible paradox of have a grandiose sense of superiority that is always seeking approval. They are continually frustrated and angry.

A driver in this last group is the most fun. He gets irate at other drivers, when all the other person has done is ignore him. This last type assumes his ideas and values about how to drive are the best and only correct way to drive. People who drive otherwise are a threat because they obviously hold different values about driving. By choosing not to see the threat, it turns into to fear—fear of being wrong. With no outlet for that fear, it turns into anger and hostility at the other drivers. This self-righteousness reinforces his sense of superiority. Now he feels justified in wanting to punish them for their misdeeds and he will engage in all sorts of ludicrous and dangerous maneuvers. These get him in all sorts of trouble, legal and otherwise, which leads to more fear and resentment.

The egocentric driver feels arrogantly superior to the driver of a lesser vehicle, envious and resentful of the person who has a better or newer car, and humiliated and embarrassed by anyone with a similar make and model. These drivers also represent one of our great reserves of racial, ethnic and cultural prejudice.

From the indications in your letter, I would place your patient the last group, which is quite common for alcoholics, although they are found in the other two groups as well. The sleepers are the ones who drive drunk and then happily drift off the side of the road, mowing down half a mile of fence posts before doing a slow-motion rollover into a ditch. The paranoid drunks, in total unawareness and with all running lights off, are frequently rear-ended while doing 25 in a 65 mile-per-hour zone. And the egocentrics, drunk or sober, will be either the cause of, or the victims in the goriest, high-speed wrecks.

I think the best approach is to keep your patient in a condition of mild, yet perpetual annoyance while in his car. Keep him out of enough danger so he is not faced with a real incentive or need to change his driving habits. You will want to assure the hours spent in self-righteousness, arrogance, and pride are immensely enjoyable and satisfying to him (and to you).

Since radios and similar devices are now common appliances in most vehicles, there are some options you will want to think about. We've done very well in the media by taking a lot of music off the air and replacing it with talk. Most of it meaningless, but we cover the whole range from truly hateful, to piously profitable. While we generally would discourage music, for its obvious connection to the Enemy, you can make inroads to pride and snobbishness through eclectic or extreme musical tastes. You can appeal to a patient's sense of aggression and hostility by engendering a preference for very loud, unpopular music. This will offend other drivers and your patient gets the satisfaction out of irritating nearly everyone around him. Plus this has the added benefit of eventual deafness. You could not ask for a better windfall than a loss of hearing to isolate your patient from other people.

Finally, try to keep your fellow oblivious that you are letting anger function with precisely the same mechanism that drove his alcohol consumption. The parallels between anger and drinking are quite remarkable. The scenario even follows a similar course. First, a justification for mild annoyance arises and your patient makes a decision and chooses to indulge in just a taste of anger. That sets him up for an opportunity to feel unjustly wronged, which undoubtedly comes along, so he gets irritable and indignant. He starts to wonder, "Why me?" This eventually snowballs from anger to fury and on to blind rage with its unquenchable desire to vent destructive retribution. The very process that used to take him from the first drink to blackout, works quite nicely with anger. I have to tell you that with some patients, it is even better than alcohol. Your patient is as powerless over the first anger as he is over the first drink. But don't let him know that.

The human who said "The road to Hell is easy"[16] said it long before there were any cars. I think we can feel quite proud of our progress in paving the way, of raising the emotional speed limit, and assuring that all along the way there is precious little of the "love and tolerance of others," which the A.A. book tries to promote in Step Ten.

Your friend,
Glumlot

Letter Twenty-One

Dear Twigmold,

The A.A. book talks about developing a "sixth sense." I assume you understand they are referring to the seldom used human capacity to directly link to the spiritual plane in a manner that allows them better contact with the Enemy. This same ability can also allow them to see us. I don't mean "see" in the visual sense to which the humans are optically limited, but to be cognizant of our presence with a degree of clarity which is most disconcerting.

We have generally done well to keep the human images of us external, large, and menacing. This is obviously preferable, for in reality it takes a very, very long time of reducing the patient to nothingness, or as close to it as possible, in order to arrive at these desired relative proportions. The commonly perceived picture is most often a manifestation of our intentions, but personified into to an imaginary physical being. In years long past, the general standard was established to divert this energy into visions of horned and red-hued demons. This strategy has been successful at keeping the humans thinking of us as separate and outside themselves on the physical dimension. By design, many find the image sufficiently unpleasant to at least consider the alternative—moving toward the Enemy. For these people, the love of God is actually fear of us[17], and the God they pursue is also a physical representation, which will always be just as inaccurate. Keep them thinking this way and the statuesque image of God, the fearful, cold, stone monolith they have contrived can be used to cast a broad shadow in which the patient can cower and shiver.

The Enemy gave the humans explicit instructions about not creating any graven images of Him. I believe He meant only to convey that it was completely impossible, so they shouldn't even waste time on such a task. But the human mental capacity is fettered by the physical, three-dimensional world. We do our best to reinforce these bonds so there is less chance of our patients breaking through to the spiritual dimension by means of the "sixth" sense.

As I touched on in my last letter, we have gotten the automobiles to serve as a graven image of the ego as God: a hard, protective exterior to keep the elements out, an internal source of considerable power, and it comes with fully self-directed control. Quite literally, the ego is in the driver's seat, which is where it wants to be. You see why men go for the sporty hot rods and big, loud trucks? And isn't the soccer-mom's minivan, waiting to burst open and spill out its cargo of writhing children really just the ultimate womb?

Since the Enemy does not allow us near the very small humans—the children—there is a tendency of most tempters to never develop an understanding of this stage of development and the significant impact it has on the ego and its relationship to God. As children, they are small, everyone else is very large. The large people seem to be in control, have answers to any question and solutions to all issues. These grownups also appear to be free of any problems, at least as the child defines problems. So an image gets fixed in the mind. As the child grows up, they use this parent image for God, but it doesn't seem to fit very well. It is further weighted down by the fact that the adults turned out to be quite irrational, unfair, and uncaring at times. This is why the cruel, punishing, and unforgiving God is still so popular.

There is the curious human phrase, "to be bigger than one's problems," which I think creates a picture of the dilemma. They learn early on that bigger was better. Big people provide food, shelter, dry diapers, and comfort. The crying child is told to be a big boy or big girl. The pre-adolescent is admonished for regressive behaviors with a condescending look and the phrase, "I thought you grew out of that." The teenager is told, "Oh, grow up." So, the solution to all problems, apparently, is to be a little bigger. Since this is not physically possible, the ego proudly marches in and says, "I can do that."

When your patient started to become alcoholic, he probably tried all sorts of methods to get the upper hand on his problem. He failed. The solution to confrontations at home or at work or on the road, was to puff himself up. That only made things worse. The ego, in its assumption of ultimate authority and responsibility, attempted to make *itself* bigger. It tried to expand its scope of power and control, because something bigger than himself was needed to overcome the obstacle facing him. Since there seemed to be nothing bigger than himself, the ego was driven to further and further extremes to offset the unacceptable possibility of failure. All of this was built on the assumption that now, as an adult, he should have all the answers, that he should always be right, that he should be bigger than his problems. It is exactly this kind of foolishness, so deeply ingrained and automatic in these humans, that is easily put to use—to keep the patient turned toward himself and away from the Enemy.

This brings me to Step Eleven, which reads in part, "Sought through prayer and meditation to improve our conscious contact with God...." Note the word *improve*. That assumes they have already developed some kind of contact with the Enemy. If you have done your job, there will be nothing for the patient to improve upon, which should render the Step ineffective. This is very important because the Step goes on to say they should pray "...only for knowledge of His will for us and the power to carry that out." That kind of simplification, especially in prayer, can make our work far more difficult than it needs to be.

You see, prayer was designed by the Enemy

specifically to help a human turn back the other way, toward the light. It is intended to help them develop their sixth sense and to facilitate a connection and communication with the spiritual plane. It is the Enemy's primary tool and in the hands of a properly skilled practitioner, it can be extremely effective. But therein lies our opportunity.

The book says that prayer works if the patient has the proper attitude and works at it. Well, there is your answer. His attitude must be a series of unrealistic, unworkable and incompatible assumptions. The work must be so intensive and exhausting that there is never enough time to do it right.

The consistent use of prayer does not come naturally nor easily to many humans. All it takes is a little attentiveness, a good sense of timing, and persistence to dislodge the patient's momentum. I am certain you covered all of the basic approaches to this in school, and given how much time was spent on it back then, one would think you would find prayer everywhere. Fortunately, this is not the case. With the A.A. folks, though, it can get a little more intense. They ought to be somewhat more motivated than the average person.

It doesn't help our cause that the instructions in the A.A. book are so specific. It says at night they are to perform a detailed self-assessment, but they are advised "...not to drift into worry, remorse or morbid reflection." Well now, just how did the human author of that passage know so much about the basic strategy taught at the training academy? Did Snuffwick let that information slip? Has the Enemy infiltrated our ranks?

In the morning they are to supposed to ask the Enemy to direct their thinking and that it be free of "...self-pity, dishonest or self-seeking motives," and when confronted with indecision, they are to ask for inspiration. They are told to "relax and take it easy."

Well, then you ought to be working at making your patient restless and uncomfortable. You need to make the whole matter of this step elaborate and complicated. If you can, you may want to get your patient excessively concerned with the rigors of the ritual. Gradually add more and more little items to the routine while holding the time allotted at a fixed constant, so that he has to start rushing through it. Imply there is some rather substantial minimum required time commitment— always more that he has available.

Use his success at work or other obligations to justify cutting his prayer time. For example, let him assume his last promotion means the boss will expect him to come in to work a little earlier and stay a little later. Tell him he has not yet found the right morning meditation book. He will spend way too much time and money browsing through bookstores looking for it.

Suggest he ought to spend more time in the morning to make a proper lunch for the kids to take to school. In the absence of that, you can suggest jogging or some other morning exercise. I personally like using the itches and twitches to distract a patient from his prayers. If the patient has developed a weekday-morning meditation routine, I find the inevitable change in patterns provided by Saturday mornings to be very good for disrupting prayer habits. This is more effective for those with young children, and it doesn't matter if the patient sleeps in late or the kids wake early. Tell him, "Well, now there's not enough time to do it right, so maybe you can get caught up tomorrow." But tomorrow there will be TV sports or yard work or children clamoring for attention, or something. Always something.

The book goes on to demand more prayer, and most of it seems intent on drawing them into the now. They are to pray for what their "next step is to be" or when they are agitated or doubtful, for the "...right thought or action." They are cautioned against the "...danger of excitement, fear, anger, worry, self-pity, or foolish decisions."

The text also suggests other spiritual affiliations are allowed. Since you haven't mentioned in your letters that your patient is a churchgoer, I can assume you have already talked him out of associating with an organized religion. If he's been mulling over attending church again, don't automatically discourage him. He would probably have a difficult time reconciling what he sees there with the new Higher Power that he now understands from his A.A. experience. Help him feel superior in the thought his God is better or more right or more compassionate or whatever and he will likely abandon the church idea altogether. With any luck, he will end up so confused that he discards all conceptions of God, thereby giving you a clean slate to work with.

Your patient may still persist in his religious interests. That's not really good, but don't think of it as bad either. It just indicates a need to change tactics. While the church is one of many paths away from us and towards the Enemy, have your man see the religiousness of the church as the end, not the means. If your man has any love of pomp and ritual, this will work. You can have him visit a denomination that he has never attended before. If it is a particularly orthodox one, he may find the ceremony and liturgy foreign and strange, and therefore probably pagan. If it is a church that has tried to modernize itself it will come across as casual and flippant.

Anyway, back to Step Eleven. Because the instructions in the book are so precise and exacting, it shouldn't take much effort to portray them as sounding oppressive and unreasonably demanding. Tell your patient the God of *his* understanding doesn't require *that* much prayer. A howdy-do in the morning ought to be enough. Besides, all the stuff in the book is man-made, right? And aren't all the other man-made trappings of religion just so much show?

Another thing to work on is to preserve the idea that his prayer and meditation time should be solemn and uninterrupted. You do this by telling him it is a very serious, precise business and he has to manage and control the environment to assure that there are absolutely no distractions. If you do this right, the sound of a passing car or even a morning birdsong will seem like an imposition on his private time. It is also important to keep him awkwardly embarrassed about being seen praying. Dress it up as sanctity if you need to, but maintain it and remind him that he could be interrupted at anytime. Someone could see him. What would they think? How would he explain it? This will keep him rushed and willing to cutting corners.

Ultimately, if you can keep him out of the book, so much the better. But your patient may be drawn to it by things he hears in meetings, from other A.A. members, or from his sponsor. Enemy agents might try to disguise an interest in the book as curiosity or as intellectual study.

If this occurs, you may want to use one of my favorite techniques. I suggest to my patient he should memorize the part of Chapter Five they read at the beginning of most meetings. He has probably heard the thing enough times that he no longer really listens, so there is little risk of any new insights. The effort expended to learn it word-for-word will waste valuable hours. If your man is a self-centered attention seeker (just a lucky guess), he will sit in meetings and lip-sync with the reading, in hopes of being observed, and therefore respected and revered as a knowledgeable authority by those newcomers who have not yet memorized it.

If he has a flair for the dramatic, let his ego seize the scene and recite Chapter Five to his bathroom mirror as if it is was Shakespearean drama, overdone accent and all. He struts his brief hour upon the stage, a walking shadow, full of sound and fury, signifying nothing, and then is heard no more.[18]

It works—it really does.

Your friend,
Glumlot

Letter Twenty-Two

Dear Twigmold,

I want to reply to your inquiry about the dog. You said in your letter the patient's young child had requested a puppy. My first reaction would be to advise against it. Like all animals, humans included, these are generally pretty disgusting creatures. If your patient inherently dislikes dogs and children, there may be a positive side to consider. The dog may bond with the child, but the tasks of cleaning up after the animal, paying the veterinary bills, filling in holes dug in the yard, putting up fencing, and so forth would all fall on the patient. Anything that adds to his frustration and imposes on "his" time, is good. The real risk in allowing him to get a dog is that these animals are able to demonstrate the nauseatingly repulsive quality called unconditional love more consistently and sincerely than most humans ever could. I admit it is unlikely your patient would be open-minded enough to actually learn such a thing from what he regards as a lower animal, but why take the risk?

There is more than enough risk in the possibility he could learn unconditional love from the practice of Step Twelve. This is one of those compound steps. It has a number of sub-components, which is good because it has the potential to confuse and complicate. The pre-dominant feature of this step is "carrying the message," which is done in a variety of ways: making coffee, attending to a treasury or the literature table, setting up chairs and so forth. You will need to make a careful assessment of your patient's aptitudes. If your fellow is the quiet, steady, and reliable background worker, he will likely be elected for a coffee or cake commitment. We want him dissatisfied with his lot, so have him see his service work as "second rate" twelfth step work. This will work specially well if he subscribes to the popular view that there is an implied status within A.A. to directly working one-on-one with other alcoholics.

As I mentioned in an earlier letter, not everybody gets the same one-hundred percent from the Enemy when they are created. I suspect it is really a quality control problem that He covers up by implying, "Oh, I meant to do that." At any rate, there are those who are better predisposed to different types of Twelfth Step work. For the service-oriented member, have him lust after the status of becoming a "guru" with a flock of devotees. If he does get started working with newcomers, hope that he gets to provide transportation for a really new one who throws up in his car. A few of these little adventures will usually persuade a patient to let his answering machine take the next call.

There is another variation to try. After he has spent a little bit of time with the newcomers, suggest that he has completed his tour of duty. You can tell him he has had his turn; he ought to let one of the newer people have a chance. If you really want to go for it, maneuver him to the assumption that he has "got it" now and needn't do any more work or read the book or go to as many meetings. This will presently lead him back to the bottle.

If he is still attending meetings, just remember the longer they're sober the harder they'll fall when they do slip. On one end of the spectrum are the perpetual newcomers who see A.A. as the drive-through fast food of sobriety. They are afraid that once they stop standing up as newcomers they will really become anonymous members of an anonymous organization. They have an infinite capacity for humiliation, but little room for humility. For the long-timer who slips, we can make coming back to the program seem impossible. It will be a bitter pill that is too large to swallow. The idea of asking for help from people who used to look up to him, implies they would now be looking down.

So how do you get your man to this point? Well, the meetings are full of great material. There's the wheezing geezer, the coffee slurper, the phlegmish cougher, and the guy who shuns showers. Have your man sit between these four on a regular basis for a while. When there is a rotation within the service committee, tell your patient the new secretary and his crew are not doing it right, or good enough, or timely. You can also have him look around while you drag up images from his first meetings. Isn't he now starting to blend in with these humorless old men? (Don't let him put together that they got old by not dying from acute alcoholism!)

I also like the deja-vu effect. While it is really a neurological phenomenon, the impact can be duplicated. It requires effort on your part, but it's often worth it. In a particularly dull meeting, comment on everything said, suggesting, "Haven't you heard that before?" Scrounge around in his memory and pull up some old pictures, preferably of unattractive people, saying the same thing he just heard. Keep at this for an hour or so, and your patient will be exhausted, tired and bored. You will be too, but no one said this would be easy. As your man complains that it's all been said before, you will want to agree, but don't let him start to think about the difference between hearing and listening.

Has your patient had to face any serious medical illnesses or accidents? These occasions often involve prescription medications that can be quite helpful—to you. Even minor colds can lead to over-the-counter medications containing alcohol. Remember the first few days of sobriety when you told your patient he would never sleep again? Try the same thing on his next really bad cold. We have rescued quite a few A.A. members with the threat of insomnia and the allure of relief from a cough medicine with a high alcohol content.

The final phrase in Step Twelve is "...practice these principles in all our affairs." The obvious question, "What principles?" First, a point of reference: all our precepts, those handed up by the Lowerarchy and Our Father Below, grow out of a single, monotheistic principle: self-centered fear. From this root grows the seven branches: esteem, acquisition, desire, retribution, appetite, ambition, and relaxation. These seven branches then intertwine to make up all the secondary motivations, which weave together into a dense canopy that shadows all things from the light.

Long ago, someone in the Enemy's camp put out some very nasty propaganda on our principles. These rumors still persist and I am certain you have heard the negative terms some humans use when referring to our seven branches. They call them the seven deadly sins. They are not sins—they are merely the tools we use to develop opportunities. I wouldn't doubt if the Enemy labels everything we do to get a patient to turn away from the light as a sin.

I once had a patient who, as part of his inventory work, started to look at our seven branches in those very terms, but I was able to sidetrack his thoughts by picturing them as the seven deadly dwarfs: Snotty, Greedy, Sleazy, Grouchy, Piggy, Whiny, and Lazy. The patient went along with my idea and assigned these names to the "committee" in his head. We even agreed that Sleazy ought to be chairman of the board.

Anyway, the Enemy's model for His principles is, of course, exceedingly complex, illogical and inconsistent. I have watched the components take shape in a patient's thoughts, and I shall do my best to describe it, or at least describe my understanding of it. At the foundation, there are only four key principles: honesty, humility, patience and generosity.

Honesty comes in a variety of forms. There is what the A.A.s call cash-register honesty. This is assumed to be based on one of the Enemy's very old mandates about not stealing, but I think it is really more a matter of generosity than honesty. Thievery is of value to us only in its potential for creating guilt, fear and remorse.

With self-honesty, there may be an infinite number of degrees. It begins with plain and obvious things one would see in a mirror. "I have this color eyes and that color skin." Not much we make of this without going to unrealistic and unsustainable extremes. With other physical attributes, like height and weight, you begin to have a little more latitude to distort the self-perception. As you move through the various stages of self-honesty, our work gets easier. If he is a pompous braggart, assure him he is just being honest in telling others the truth about his long list of accomplishments. If he is cruel and sarcastic, we convince him that he has been gifted with a sharp and clever wit, but is saddled with the misfortune of being surrounded by humorless dolts.

Finally there is spiritual honesty, which is really quite rare. It is based on the accuracy in a human's perception of the relationship between himself and the Enemy. It is built on a foundation of the other types of honesty. Therefore, distort the little things wherever you can and have the patient keep at least one dark corner for your exclusive use.

Humility, in its true form, is not when a human has an artificially low opinion of himself or his talents. It is when he does not think about himself at all. But to do this he would have to be thinking about someone or something else. Well, that is precisely what the Enemy would like to see and this may be the idea behind A.A.'s twelfth step. If your fellow is "getting out of himself" by working with others or doing the menial service tasks, then he may be starting to develop some humility. The best defense against this is to suggest that since he has become so knowledgeable and experienced at practicing humility, he ought to be regarded an expert. Once you convince him of this, then tell him it is only his humility that keeps him from demanding his due respect and recognition, and that he is certainly justified in feeling annoyed at all those obviously self-centered people in his group who continually withhold praise.

Generosity should always be defined for your patient in purely financial terms. The economic principle of fair market value should be the only gauge in considering any transaction. For example, if a patient has a surplus of money or material goods, sharing a small portion of the excess is sufficient to warrant being called "a generous fellow." Giving a little spare change to a homeless person on occasion is worth lots of points in the Enemy's ledger of good deeds. An extra dollar or two in the A.A. basket is a very noble gesture, as long as gets noticed. But generous with his time? Where is the trade off in that kind of deal? If it's not win-win, then forget it. Generous in allowing other people to be wrong? No sense in him wasting time to explore that. Keep his thinking restricted along these lines and he will never get close to considering that generosity of spirit is really what the Enemy values.

Patience is a quality somewhat peculiar to the phenomenon of terrestrial time, and is exemplified by the most basic form—deferred gratification. In its higher application, patience is the willing postponement of expectations and emotional commitments regarding any given future situation to that point in time when such events become "now." You see, the Enemy always wants the humans to be with Him, which is in the present moment. The whole business of human existence requires occasional thoughts about the future, dealing with planning and anticipating outcomes. But since a human cannot be in the future successfully, the Enemy recommends patience as a form of acceptance. I imagine it is similar to what I once overheard a human parent telling his anxious child, "It's not then yet."

Our best work is done by having the humans pay dearly, very dearly with all-consuming fear and worry about what might happen tomorrow. Even hope or excitement, as long as it is excessive and futile, is beneficial to us. In either case, it squanders emotional energy on unreal events, while providing nothing of any value whatsoever to the patient. The person ends up exhausted, disappointed or both.

I have invested a lot of time and effort observing how these four principles—honest, humility, generosity and patience—are manifested in a human mind. You must remember that they live in the physical world, which was assembled according to the Enemy's own mathematical rules. So, imagine if you will, that each of these four principles is a point in a three-dimensional geometric configuration. Now this is where it gets really silly and the whole logic of the Enemy's ridiculous scheme starts to unravel. Supposedly, there are links between each of the four points that create six additional principles: trust, faith, forgiveness, courage, hope and kindness. The boundaries of these six then combine to form charity, gratitude, sincerity and sobriety. Finally, as far as I can tell, all of these principles exist as components of one grand equation that is something like: love equals truth and truth equals love.

Isn't that bizarre? And most certainly it is all impossible. This further supports my theory that these principles, and the rest of what the Enemy claims as His truths, are all a smokescreen to cover up His *real* scheme. The Enemy is in this for the same thing we are. He has to be. Why else would He? Since we know how easy it is to confuse the humans, I guess we can't really blame the Enemy for doing the very same thing we do. As a matter of fact, it is probably a compliment to our methods.

Will your patient practice these principles in all his

affairs? Well, I think I have just shown they are all built on quicksand, so I frankly wouldn't give it too much thought. Besides, the A.A. book gives its members an "out" where it says that none of them has been able to maintain anything like perfect adherence to the principles. Tell him, "See, nobody is perfect—so why even waste the effort?"

One human said it for us, "It is easier to fight for principles than live up to them."[19] So, if your patient does get inspired about Step Twelve, let him become the self-appointed, self-righteous, puritanical and militant defender of the Twelve Traditions for his group. This just about guarantees that, if nothing else, he will be very much alone.

Your friend,
Glumlot

Letter Twenty-Three

Dear Twigmold

I did want to fire off a letter to you and tell you what happened to Snuffwick. This version isn't widely circulated, so I dare not say if it is accurate or not. I would not want to be quoted as saying anything true, now, would I? That would be very bad for my reputation.

Some tempters think there are prime assignments across the ages that are especially easy or entertaining. For example, I'm sure you've heard that attending to a Roman Catholic cleric in the middle ages is usually pretty amusing; as is being assigned a televangelist in the late 20th century. And there are those who hold that the simplest task of all is securing the soul of a pre-A.A. drunkard.

Snuffwick was a party to exactly such a debate among a group of academicians. He proposed that drunks were so easy to work with that he could do two at once if it were allowed. When one of the others challenged him on this, Snuffwick offered to come out of retirement to prove his point if someone could get a waiver to the rules. There was some political wrangling but the stakes were high enough and someone in the Lowerarchy (who is rumored to have had a piece of the action) approved the dual assignment.

Two alcoholics were picked at random, but since the wager was "two at *one time*," they were in the same temporal position, although geographically separated. One was a New York stock speculator and the other was a physician from Akron, Ohio. All went quite well for Snuffwick for a long while. Both were chronic drunks and were progressing quite nicely with deteriorating health and intractable business problems. The New Yorker, whom we shall call Bill, was just about done for, when he was approached by an old friend who had gone religious. Bill was put off by this, but an Enemy agent suggested since everything else had failed, why not try it? Bill headed for the detoxification hospital and there was the alleged incident where the Enemy appeared. We have Bill's account of what happened, but it is pretty unbelievable stuff. For obvious reasons, we have no reliable firsthand reports of such encounters with that blinding light and deafening silence.

Anyway, out of his experience, Bill was beginning to stay away from alcohol again. He got the idea (probably from an Enemy agent) that he could help other drunks to have the same experience. Fortunately, Snuffwick pushed Bill to the extremes of self-righteousness, so no-one was very interested in Bill's preaching of a spectacular spiritual experience. When Bill went to visit his doctor, Dr. Silkworth, at the hospital, Snuffwick was on the lookout for another fancy theatrical performance by the Enemy. Instead, it seems one of the

Enemy's agents had gotten hold of Silkworth. The physician suggested that Bill ought to emphasize the medical aspects of the illness first, then bring in the spiritual stuff.

Attempting to drive Bill back to drinking, Snuffwick got him involved in some utterly hopeless business deals, one of which took him to Akron. Snuffwick managed to keep his two patients on separate paths almost the whole time. With the business deal failing disastrously, Bill was just about to walk into the bar at the Mayfair Hotel, when the course of events turned. Bill was directed (by the Enemy, no doubt) to seek out a person who, by coincidence, knew Snuffwick's other patient—the Akron physician. This doctor, whom we shall call Dr. Bob, was just as bad as Bill, but had kept his medical practice going somehow. A meeting was arranged between the two men, and Dr. Bob took Snuffwick's suggestion to consent to the meeting only if it was limited to fifteen minutes, and no longer. Well, six hours later, unknown to Bill or Dr. Bob, Alcoholics Anonymous had started.

Snuffwick was in over his head now, and he was outnumbered by Enemy agents. Bill started writing a book, and Snuffwick did his best to muddle up the text. The story goes that the light was so bright at the writing of the Steps, Snuffwick may have suffered permanent damage. He kept at his post, trying to steer his two patients off track. He tried disorganizing the groups, suggesting they turn their organizational chart upside down. Rather than creating a problem, the idea was successfully incorporated into the structure.

Snuffwick hung on until the end, but evenutally both patients were lost to the Enemy. The doctor left first, laughing at Snuffwick, seeing through his plans and designs to complicate the program. The doctor's parting shot was an admonition to Bill to "keep it simple." Bill lived for another 21 years, all of it devoted Alcoholics Anonymous.

As you well know, their "simple program" has made our work unnecessarily difficult, and has snatched away countless thousands of what would have been otherwise easily acquired souls. We had assumed the Enemy would concede that some "acceptable losses" are simply part the price of war. But no. He has found a way to recruit the worst cases, the furthest lost, the totally hopeless, to retrieve other drunks from the final precipice. And it started with one drunk talking to another, carrying a message of hope and the promise of freedom.

This is why it is no longer allowed for tempters to take on more than one patient concurrently, and subsequent assignments are never in close temporal or geographical proximity. Snuffwick is now a perpetual condiment at the table of Our Father Below. Like a bottomless salt shaker, he will be internally, eternally and infernally savored and consumed in the total and incomprehensible darkness. So, that is Snuffwick's story as I heard it.

As discouraging as the whole A.A. phenomenon might seem, we can learn from these people. We can "Keep coming back"—persistence and perseverance are essential for our success. "Easy does it"—avoid the overly dramatic. Stay with the slow, steady methods. "Let go and let God"—sit back and allow the patient's prejudice and fears of religious and spiritual ideas interfere with his progress.

We have to accept the challenges that come with having a patient in A.A. We have to make a decision that we are not going to give up. We ought to admit our mistakes, correct them, learn from them and move on. And I believe that we, as tempters, can do more to help ourselves by learning from each other. When we see a tempter making the same mistakes that we have made, we ought to be able to show him what we have done, and to simply lay out the kit of tools for his inspection. If he is not interested, we can go find another tempter who wants what we have.

Your friend,
Glumlot

P.S. I did mention in one of letters that it would be best to *not* pass along my correspondence to anyone else in the Lowerarchy, right? There are undervisors who would read these letters and come to the entirely wrong conclusion about my methods and motivations. I do appreciate your handling these confidentially.

Letter Twenty-Four

Dear Twigmold,

I want to thank you for the regular correspondence. I immensely enjoyed our communications, and I hope you were able to get something out if it. I know that sharing my experience, strength and hope with you has helped me in my work with alcoholics. Who knows—maybe you have helped me more than I helped you!

I am aware that you have been under considerable pressure concerning your quota. I am sure that if you apply yourself, you can find something in my notes that will be of some help. I have always sensed your determination and firmly believe your willingness to "go to any length" will assure that you will find a way to put this information to good use in attaining your success.

Unfortunately, I must tell you that I may not be writing to you again for a while. There hasn't been any official announcement of this, so I guess you get to be the first to know: I just recently got the word that I am being given a new *permanent* assignment.

No more temptation duty! Just think of it. Gone are the endless hours poised at a patient's ear, waiting for the next opportunity to make a suggestion, to twist the incoming messages, to reinforce the faulty assumptions.

No more of those tedious and unbearable conditions. No more music, no more Enemy agents, and no more A.A. meetings. But best of all—no more laughter. If you ever had any question about how much animal nature the Enemy gave these humans, just listen to them laugh. It is absolutely the most disgusting thing. They grunt and snort and gasp and howl.   No. I shall not miss that at all.

I wish I could tell you more about my new position, but someone down in the Lowerarchy decided to keep the particular details of my new duties a surprise. I don't mean to criticize the bureaucrats, but they often make the biggest deals out of nothing. However, given the level of secrecy surrounding this, I can only guess that this must really be quite a significant honor. So, if they want to play it up, well, that's fine with me.

What I do know, and what makes it even more special, is that in recognition of the event, I have been personally invited to a private ceremony and banquet being held down (way, way down—I might add) in the Lowerarchy. I confess that I am so excited that I have not yet fully digested the whole idea.

Oh, I do wish you could be there to see me!

Forever yours,
Glumlot

Appendix I

Quotation and reference sources

1. Robert Ingersoll, 1833-1899, American Lawyer and Orator, *Some Mistakes of Moses* (1879).
2. Unknown.
3. Gerald May, *Addiction and Grace*, p 102 (HarperCollins Books 1988).
4. Gerald May, ibid, p 105.
5. A member of Alcoholics Anonymous.
6. Blaise Pascal, 1623-1662, French mathematician and philosopher, *Pensées* (1670).
7. Fred B , from an A.A. talk in 1989, Palos Verdes, CA.
8. Virginia Woolf, 1882-1941, British writer, *The Moment and other Essays*, (pub 1948).
9. Fyodor Dostoyevsky, 1821-1881, Russian novelist, *The Brothers Karamozov* (1880).
10. Jonathan Bernstein, 1951-, Business Consultant, from a conversation in 1994.
11. Henry Kissinger, 1923-, Former U.S. Secretary of State, from an interview in *Esquire Magazine*, June 1975.
12. Hannah More, 1745-1883, British religious writer.
13. William Congreve, British playwright, 1670-1729, *The Mourning Bride*, 1697.
14. Jessamyn West, 1902-1984, American author.
15. William James, 1842-1910, American psychologist and philosopher, *Pragmatism*, 1907.
16. Virgil, 70-19 B.C., Roman Poet, *The Aeneid* 19 B.C.
17. Voltaire, 1694-1778, French philosopher, *The Philosophical Dictionary*, 1764.
18. William Shakespeare, 1564-1616, *MacBeth*.
19. Alfred Adler, 1870-1937, Austrian psychologist, *Problems of Neurosis* 1929.

Appendix II

The Twelve Steps of Alcoholics Anonymous

1. We admitted we were powerless over alcohol — that our lives had become unmanageable.
2. Came to believe that a Power greater than ourselves could restore us to sanity.
3. Made a decision to turn our will and our lives over to the care of God *as we understood Him*.
4. Made a searching and fearless moral inventory of ourselves.
5. Admitted to God, to ourselves, and to another human being the exact nature of our wrongs.
6. Were entirely ready to have God remove all these defects of character.
7. Humbly asked Him to remove our shortcomings.
8. Made a list of all persons we had harmed, and became willing to make amends to them all.
9. Made direct amends to such people wherever possible, except when to do so would injure them or others.
10. Continued to take personal inventory and when we were wrong promptly admitted it.
11. Sought through prayer and meditation to improve our conscious contact with God *as we understood Him*, praying only for knowledge of His will for us and the power to carry that out.
12. Having had a spiritual awakening as the result of these steps, we tried to carry this message to alcoholics, and to practice these principles in all our affairs.

Alcoholics Anonymous, pgs 59-60.

Appendix III

Other References to the "Big Book" of Alcoholics Anonymous

Credits and Kudos

A Gratitude List

I wish to thank all those who made this book possible through their contributions of encouragement, ideas, guidance, inspiration, patience, technical assistance, friendship, understanding and support:

Alan B, Alex F, Augie S, Bill W & Dr.Bob, Bob McC, Chris H, Chuck & Vivian, Dan F, Dick P, Dr. Paul O, Frank F, Gerry McD, Herb K, James F, Jim R, Jim W, Joe McQ & Charlie P, John O'D, Jonathan & Celeste, Kevin J, Kritika & Dhyana, Larry C, Larry J, Larry S, Lee R, Leland W, LizAnn A, Luis O, Mike H, Mike O, Milt L, Nick J, Ron McC, Steve & Guy, and Sylvia L.

My sincere gratitude also goes to all who, by showing up for their own lives, have enriched mine, making it a far better life than I could have ever imagined. Thank you.

Finally, I think God had something to do with this project. I hope and pray that I can be worthy of the gifts He asks me to share, and that I may honor Him with faith and willingness to live in the sunlight of the spirit.

— Stanley M.

Additional copies of *The Glumlot Letters* are available for $12.00 each. California residents please add $1.00 for sales tax. U.S. Postage and handling is $4.00 for Priority Mail or $2.50 for standard mail. Checks or money orders payable to South Bay Books.

(1997 prices and rates, subject to change without notice)

mail to:
SOUTH BAY BOOKS
PO Box 3272
Torrance, CA 90510-3272

For credit card orders call TOLL FREE:
1-888 5 books 5
(1-888-526-6575)

or visit our web site:
www.southbaybooks.com

A portion of the profits from the sale of the book, *The Glumlot Letters,* is donated to help support recovery homes for men and women alcoholics.